# Collected
# Management
# Wisdom

~ Stratford Managers Corporation ~

Illustrations by Yvonne Craig-Isfan and Jo-Ann Pullen
Cover Design by Jo-Ann Pullen

ISBN: 1468010859
ISBN-13: 9781468010855

## Introduction

Once upon a time, a group of highly experienced business executives from a variety of management disciplines, banded together to form a consulting firm called Stratford Managers. This firm was different from other consulting firms because the people there were practitioners, not consultants. They coached their clients from the perspective of peers and climbed down into the trenches with them to help improve their businesses.

Along the way, the folks at Stratford Managers dispensed a lot of advice and told a lot of stories. These stories were captured in a blog that developed quite a following. This book is a collection of the best blog posts from 2010 and 2011, although the management wisdom contained within them is timeless.

Business is a passion for Stratford Managers. They are an intense bunch that works hard but likes to have a little fun. Though they cover serious business topics, their "joie d'affaires" comes through in the writings and illustrations in this collection. In fact, this book is sort of an executive MBA course, but with cartoons.

If after dipping into this book you want to continue your education, visit www.stratfordmanagers.com/blog and subscribe to the weekly post from their "Collected Management Wisdom" blog.

# Table of Contents

# I.
# Management

## *One Afternoon in Shanghai*

A common challenge for growing businesses is keeping their diverse locations working together effectively. There are many barriers to collaboration between staff that are scattered all over the world: culture, time zones and even language. It's particularly hard when a company grows through international acquisition and there isn't even a shared corporate history to knit the organization together.

Often it falls to the regional offices to make the effort to stay connected to headquarters. In my many years working for multi-national companies I have always had great respect for the herculean attempts made by staff in Asia to work effectively with the "mother ship" in North America. Constant late-night conference calls after long days of work. Calling in from vacations. Suffering through long international flights to attend meetings. All this on top of the challenge of working in the geographically enormous and culturally diverse business environment that is Asia.

That's why I was so impressed by a recent initiative by one company's Shanghai-based staff to help bridge the divide with their co-workers in Canada. In the words of the originator in Shanghai, "*Communication barriers by different languages exist forever, however we never give up trying to understand others better! As a global organization, how much we understand one another determines the efficiency of operations. From our side, many people in Shanghai desire to know and understand the language and culture of foreign friends more and better, and we think one of the keys to improve this is to listen more.*" His idea is brilliantly simple: every time a colleague from North America arrives, the visitor is asked to deliver a short presentation to tell a story to local employees.

This voluntary program provides opportunities for Shanghai staff to learn the culture and language of their colleagues from North America. Stories can be on any topic: someone's hometown, a festival or tradition, a favorite sport … whatever. After spending 15 minutes talking, the presenter asks the audience three questions so they can work on their English speaking skills.

I give full credit to these employees for taking the initiative to improve their language skills and for developing a creative way to connect at a human level with their North American colleagues. It says a lot about their enthusiasm, motivation and ambition. I doubt a North American branch-office would do the same.

If your company has global offices, what are you doing to help bridge cultural, language and geographic gaps? The first step might be as simple as telling a story.

~ Doug Michaelides ~

## *People-Centered Companies*

I recently visited a fast growing company with nearly 300 employees. As I entered, a friendly, cheerful receptionist greeted me. Since I was a bit early, I sat in the lobby admiring the decorations. Team pictures and recognition awards of all sorts covered the wall. I also noticed the receptionist was putting together nice frames containing employee service award certificates.

The CEO walked me through the office and I was impressed that she knew everyone by name, speaking with them as peers. Everyone seemed happy and working hard. They explained their work to me with enthusiasm and pride.

When I commented on the positive culture, the CEO described several team building activities the company runs, some as simple as playing mini-golf in the hallways of the building. These activities take just an hour but gather employees together for a good laugh and a little friendly competition. It reminded me that team building exercises don't need to be elaborate, expensive off-site affairs.

Any activity that encourages interaction between groups that may not normally work together on a daily basis helps to build culture across the company. The key is to do it consistently without waiting for the excuse of a big milestone or achievement. Focusing on the people as well as the product releases provides positive results for both company and employees!

It is important for employees to feel valued and empowered so they dare to try new things. Even though their attempts may not result in immediate success, employees will learn and grow from their experiences. Supporting their efforts to take risks, and accepting periodic failures, is as important to new employees as encouraging a baby to walk knowing that occasionally she will fall!

After my short tour, it didn't surprise me to learn that this company is doing rather well. By focusing on its people and making them feel important and empowered, the company has created a culture where every employee believes they can make a difference. As a result, they actually do. It reminded me of the "good old days" at Newbridge Networks, where I was lucky enough to work for several years.

My first boss at Newbridge always told me I would be more rewarded for trying and failing than for not trying at all, as long as I learned through failure to reach higher levels of knowledge and confidence. He was a wise man (and still is!).

~ Natalie Giroux ~

## *Mean What You Say*

The other day I was having lunch with a former colleague. We had been through some tough times together at a previous employer so I was looking forward to catching up and learning about his latest successes. We had a nice chat then, over coffee, he reached into his jacket and pulled out a sheaf of papers. "This is my last performance review from when I worked for you", he said. "Do you think you could explain a couple of things for me?"

I racked my brains. The date on the document showed that I had prepared the review several years ago but I had no clear recollection. Fortunately, the two points he wanted to talk about I remembered quite well so we had a good talk – sort of an impromptu, post-game debriefing. All the pressures and politics of "the game" we were embroiled in at the time had evaporated so it was easy to have an open discussion. Afterwards in an email thanking me he said, "I wish I had been more open to your guidance when we were working together. More than ever I know what I want from work, what I thrive on, where I can find both …"

Wow! So often, when we do performance reviews, we're not sure why we bother. We take them seriously because they can influence compensation but sometimes it feels like we're just going through the motions of some corporate administrative process. Over my career, I must have prepared hundreds of them. And every last one is written down and stored somewhere, a permanent judgment on someone and a lasting legacy of my actions as a manager!

I have a friend who advised his teenage daughter when she started going out on the town, "Don't do anything you wouldn't want to read about in tomorrow's newspaper". The same applies to performance reviews. That doesn't mean shying away from honest, constructive feedback. But you better make sure you are being objective and can substantiate your point of view. You should be writing a Pulitzer prize-winning story, not a gossip column!

I'll bet if I had known that one day, a colleague would call me out of the blue and hold me accountable for what I had written in a performance review, I'd have worked a little harder on them all. What about you?

~ Doug Michaelides ~

## *Managing Performance vs. Objectives*

It's the time of year when many of us are setting objectives – for ourselves (New Year's resolutions) and for others (MBOs). Being mostly Type-A, results-oriented people, the concept of setting objectives is deeply engrained.

Actually, the whole discipline of Management by Objectives (MBOs) is an outcome of the corporation's responsibility to deliver income and profits to its owners and shareholders. This commitment to a hard deliverable cascades down through the rest of the organization every financial cycle. The only problem is that we're dealing with people, and people are notoriously bad at setting and meeting objectives.

Think about your own New Year's resolutions. A couple weeks or so into the new year, how many of them have you already given up for lost? What is your track record from previous years? Many of us don't even make New Year's resolutions anymore. Why bother? They mostly remain unachieved and we end up feeling bad about ourselves because we've failed. The same issue applies in the workplace.

A better approach is to focus a little less on objectives and a little more on behavior. Your performance is something you can change and if you blow it one day you get another crack at it the next. By connecting the right behavior or performance metrics to the desired objectives, you ensure that the changes in how the work is performed will yield the desired results (after all, it is ultimately the results that we're after). Let's call it Management by Performance (MBP).

I'm not suggesting abandoning objective-setting altogether. But let's acknowledge that what's important isn't the setting of objectives but rather the achievement of results. If your personal or corporate MBO process isn't delivering results, it's crazy not to complement it with a performance-based, behavioral approach. Give it a try with an employee who has had trouble meeting objectives (or with objectives that everyone has had trouble meeting!).

By the way, that's what coaches do all the time. They help you focus on modifying your behavior with the intent of improving your results. Neat trick, huh?

So, before it is too late, change your New Year's resolution! Don't set a goal of losing 10 pounds by March 1. Instead, resolve to eat more vegetables and cut out the second drink after work. The change in behavior might just actually deliver the results you've been striving to achieve.

~ Doug Michaelides ~

## *Are You Level Conscious?*

We all know there is a hierarchy in any organization. We hope this hierarchy is related to competency. One dimension of management competency that really matters has to do with the ability to scale one's thinking.

At the lowest level, an individual is required to focus on a **task**. His challenge is simply to avoid distractions (work, friends, social media or otherwise) and complete his work on time with satisfactory quality.

The next level up the chain puts these tasks in the context of a **project** - a series of interrelated activities that result in a larger outcome. The longer the timeline and the more tasks involved, the more sophisticated the individual needs to be in their ability to manage.

The next rung up the management ladder is concerned about the **plan** that initiates all these projects. The plan coordinates multiple projects in order to achieve a higher-order objective that may have wider impact outside his functional area. It's no longer just about what needs to get done but why it needs to be done.

At the top of the stack is the person who is responsible for the **strategy** that spawned all the plans. She is the person who leads the translation of external factors into internal initiatives. She is steeped in "why" rather than "how".

Obviously this is a simplified view of organizational reality but the model is useful in a number of ways. First, it helps you calibrate your expectations from different levels in the organization and prepares you to provide the right type of coaching so each person can succeed. It also helps you identify those individuals who have mastered the competencies at their current level and are ready to step up to the next. Finally, by understanding the competency hierarchy in the organization, you can more easily isolate the points of failure that are interfering with achieving corporate goals.

As a final note, keep watch for those rare people who can move easily between multiple competency levels (ie. who can think strategically, pull together a plan, manage a project and focus on getting individual tasks done). These are your "go-to" people when you're faced with major opportunities or threats.

By the way, just because there are multiple levels in the organization doesn't mean one is better than another. Employees contributing at all levels are required for the organization to succeed (though in smaller organizations multiple levels can be compressed into those "go-to" people I just mentioned).

Here's a little career planning game: place yourself in this hierarchy. What skills do you need to develop to take the next step?

~ Doug Michaelides ~

## *Deciding To Decide*

Does your company or management team have trouble making decisions? At the pace of business these days, an inability to make timely decisions can be fatal. It can also be a cause of frustration for everyone involved (including employees counting on the management team for direction).

So why do smart people have problems making decisions? Here are a few things to watch out for:

**Nobody's in charge.** Is it clear who is responsible for the decision? If not, endless debate can ensue without concrete actions.

**Too many cooks in the kitchen**. While everyone has an opinion, not all opinions must be considered equally. One person can easily decide where to go for lunch. Two people can probably negotiate an acceptable compromise. Three people (or more) may end up going hungry for lack of consensus!

**Communication by email.** Email is often an enemy of communication since it is a linear process. An email thread easily turns into a tangle of misunderstanding and asynchronous confusion particularly when multiple people are involved. Email also lengthens the decision-making process because it is non-real-time. Better to talk through a decision and then use email to document it.

**Seeking perfection.** Rarely is a decision a "life and death" matter. The quality of a decision generally improves as more information is gathered up to a point of diminishing returns. Most of the time it is better to err on the side of rapid action, before the window of opportunity closes, than to suffer the costs of dragging a decision on too long. There will usually be a chance to optimize your decision later if necessary and there are certainly plenty more waiting to be made. Who has the time and resources to linger painfully on each one?

**It's not a competition.** Most senior management teams are full of strong personalities. Getting their way is how they've climbed to the top. When group decision-making becomes a competition between personalities your management team is in trouble. Even the smartest most talented managers need to know when to lead and when to follow.

**Commitment.** Making a decision involves taking a risk. Not everyone is willing to put their reputation (and perhaps their job) on the line by taking a stand. What about you?

Businesses and careers are powered by decisions. Individuals and organizations that are unwilling or unable to make decisions will die a slow and painful death. So, why not make the decision right now to create a culture of action within your management team?

~ Doug Michaelides ~

## *Why I Shouldn't Hire Jim Roche*

A little while ago I was waiting for a delayed flight in a crowded lounge. Across from me, two men were working on a presentation. It was apparent that the fellow on the left worked for the guy on the right. They were both stocky with thick necks and short hair. They wore jeans, cowboy boots and black mock-turtlenecks. They even used similar gestures.

Last week I was getting into an elevator behind two gentlemen talking about a maintenance problem. They were of similar height and both had handlebar mustaches, open windbreakers and two-way radios in their right hands. They were speaking English, with a thick French accent. The guy who got on first was the boss.

These two examples are illustrative of a management pitfall that stems from a common human tendency. We are more comfortable with the familiar. We inadvertently tend to hire people like ourselves.

In his book <u>Blink</u>, Malcolm Gladwell cites the example of how musician Abby Conant won a competition for first trombone in the Munich Philharmonic, much to the surprise of the all-male selection committee. As a woman, without the blind behind which everyone auditioned, she would probably not have been chosen. This is not just gender discrimination; it reflects an unconscious bias to which we can all fall victim.

Another illustration of unconscious bias was a recent study in which researchers created two different resumes depicting similar skills. Both were sent to Canadian companies with job openings. The resume with the anglicized name got a call back far more frequently than the one with the foreign-sounding name. I doubt that many of the resume screeners were conscious of their slanted actions.

Hiring people like ourselves is a management pitfall because homogeneity can lead to groupthink. The best teams are cohesive, but diverse in the character, background and experience. This diversity leads to richer conversations, a broader spectrum of ideas and ultimately to better decisions. That's why I shouldn't hire Jim Roche. Instead I should look for people who have a different make-up than mine.

A powerful tool for helping build diversity is the Myers-Briggs Type Indicator (MBTI). It is easy to learn and surprisingly effective. I try to avoid pigeonholing, but I do use the MBTI as a framework for thinking about teams.

Other obvious ways to increase team diversity include looking for different cultural backgrounds, finding a balance among men and women, bringing on people with different work experiences, or looking for people with strong passions that are complementary to the rest of the team.

Not only will these practices lead to better decisions and better business results, they will also lead to teams that offer a richer social experience. I would hate to spend all day talking to myself!

~ Jim Roche ~

## *Projects or Proposals? Which Ones Get the Resources?*

Competing demands on resources to support both new business opportunities and ongoing project deliveries can be a significant challenge for professional services firms, especially during periods of business growth.

As a senior delivery manager, have you ever wondered how to complete all of those proposals in time while maintaining current project schedules? Do you live in fear of not being able to deliver all of the new business successfully if you win too many bids? This dilemma faces professional services organizations of every size and stage of growth sooner or later.

Resource management must be carefully planned to ensure client satisfaction as well as that of the company stakeholders. In my first professional services sales role many years ago, I was once told not to worry about how we would deliver the business I won, since project delivery was someone else's problem. It was later in my career as a delivery manager that I came to appreciate the complexity of resource management and growth planning, along with its impact on the bottom line.

Senior management including sales, delivery, human resources and finance all need to be in alignment on the company's resource planning and execution approach to mitigate the risk of under-performing project deliveries or mediocre proposals. Holding regular cross-functional resourcing meetings and matching the hiring funnel to the sales funnel are key elements of a successful resource management strategy. Customer satisfaction is earned through the consistent delivery of project commitments, which leads to the coveted follow-on business opportunities that all professional services firms cherish.

So as your company plans for growth in the coming year, consider adding this topic to the agenda of your annual planning session and be prepared for the success that is coming!

~ Brian Campagnola ~

## Managing High-Powered But Short-Lived Projects

In the Feb. 25, 2010 issue of the Economist magazine, an article entitled "Joining the Queue" about recruiting firms stated:

*". . . Manpower [Inc.] is increasingly having to . . . help recruiters . . . manage high-powered but short-lived projects. Companies are putting together many more ad hoc teams often connected virtually around the world, notes Mr. Joerres [CEO of Manpower Inc.]. "Perhaps only 20% of a team will be on the full-time staff," he says, "so they need a much more on-demand talent spigot . . ."*

I'm not an HR expert but it seems to me that "on-demand" talent is an idea whose time has come for a few reasons:

1. Many companies coming out of the recession remain intentionally lean as a hedge against future uncertainty. This presents an obstacle to tackling new opportunities.
2. An aging (i.e. retiring) workforce means that the depth of experience required to manage high-powered, business critical projects is in short supply.
3. Communications and collaboration technology makes it increasingly easy to knit together project teams of internal and external resources stretching across large geographic areas.

Most managers are familiar with hiring contractors to provide more "horsepower" for project delivery. This has long been a common practice in the IT industry. However as the HR issue has shifted from a shortage of workers to a shortage of experience and talent, more companies are engaging experienced outside consultants to provide leadership for projects as well as coaching for internal resources.

Consultants that provide hands-on management services can overcome the "experience gap" and get important projects off the ground without the need for a long-term employment commitment. An added benefit is that a company's middle management receives training and development during project implementation. These employees recognize that coaching from a senior consultant is an investment in their professional development, which helps with the retention of top talent.

The conclusion? Resourceful companies don't let a lack of resources become an obstacle to achieving business objectives!

~ Doug Michaelides ~

# II.
# Leadership

## Management By Sitting Around

You've heard of the well-known management practice of "management by walking around"? A fascinating variant I learned from a local CEO is something I call "management by sitting around".

This CEO, newly installed at the helm of a struggling 40-person company, instituted a "mini-ops" meeting to accelerate his understanding of the business and establish his relationship with employees. During these meetings, all working-level staff, from the receptionist to developers, deliver an update to the CEO with their colleagues as a silent audience. The management team is also required to simply sit and listen.

Everyone gets their 15 minutes of fame, presenting just 3 slides: a summary of the past period, plans for the current period, and challenges they face. In a company with 25-30 non-management presenters, the meeting takes a full day. The mini-ops reviews started out monthly but as the company stabilized moved to a quarterly pace.

At first, many employees were terrified and resistant. It was the first time many of them had ever presented (let alone to the CEO!). But for the CEO, it was a way to see potential leaders in action, have issues raised more directly, and keep a sugarcoating management team honest.

The CEO sets the tone for these meetings by remaining relentlessly positive and focusing on opportunities for improvement. He admitted that the first couple of sessions were a bit rocky but before long the bad news and big opportunities (the stuff he really wanted to hear) began to come out. To sustain this openness concrete action must be taken on issues that are raised. Just because you're sitting around, doesn't mean you can be lazy!

As an added benefit, open communication also breaks down organizational barriers. The CEO recounted that after the office manager presented, the office gradually grew cleaner. Everyone began doing their part to keep things tidy.

All-staff presentations become unwieldy once the company reaches about 50 people. At that point, splitting the meeting between a couple of top executives and employee groups might be a good idea. Also consider other informal variations on "management by sitting around". For example, this CEO occasionally joins some of his staff in the lunchroom while they play cards. There's no business talk allowed but somehow if there's an issue, it gets raised.

The principle of giving working-level employees a direct channel to the top is sound. But it can't be lip service or you'll just keep hearing what everyone thinks you want to hear. It may be less exercise, but enlightened managers may discover that sitting around with their staff can be just as effective as the more active alternative!

~ Doug Michaelides ~

## *The Vision Thing*

In the recent British Open Championship, Darren Clarke was asked if he ever thought he'd be in the winner's circle again at the age of 42. His response was, "Of course. I always had the vision".

All professional golfers stand behind the ball and visualize it going exactly where they want. Is this just wishful thinking? Undoubtedly the shot doesn't always happen precisely as planned, but then imagining the ball going into the water hazard wouldn't exactly help either. In golf, as in work and life in general, to achieve really positive results it's important to imagine the best outcome.

I've known or followed a number of CEOs in my career. The successful ones, and the ones who were the most fun to work with, had the clearest vision of what success meant to them. They held their vision up for all to see and made it very clear where they were going and what needed to be done to get there.

Of course there were always obstacles along the way to achieving their goals, but overcoming the bumps in the road helped everyone recognize that progress was being made. Was the original vision always achieved? Not necessarily. But as long as they weren't tilting at windmills (it's a fine line sometimes), the clarity of purpose invariably yielded success in some form. As Terry Matthews says, "If I can live with the worst then I'll plan for the best".

In your work, are you more inclined to imagine the project or campaign you're working on failing or succeeding? How does your frame of mind affect the outcome of your endeavors? When planning for success, it is best to write down your desired outcomes as a commitment to yourself to continually strive to make them happen.

How about in your life and career? Do you think clearly about where you want to be in five or ten years? Having a vision helps guide your actions towards your destination. Although your idea of success may evolve along the way, once the general direction is set, a positive outcome becomes within your reach.

~ Sandra Pacey ~

## *What's Your Back-Up Plan?*

As I sit in my home office working with the roar of a generator in the background, I'm pretty frustrated with the latest power outages in my neighborhood. This isn't the first time either. A few months ago, we were without electricity for more than 14 hours. At least I wasn't alone. There were over 40,000 homes and businesses in the region without power because a storm blew out a transformer. So here I am again, in the middle of a windstorm not knowing when the power will be restored. And I am working to a deadline that cannot change.

Growing up in a rural community taught me about managing through winter storms, power outages, water shortages, and whatever else nature or bad luck decides to throw at you. So I always have a back-up plan of some sort. Some people think that planning for the worst is just planning for failure. I don't agree. I think it's about being prepared and resourceful; about having contingency plans and being ready to figure things out on the fly.

Over my career I've had many "power disruptions" thrown my way. These were circumstances caused by events outside my control – everything from website failures and crisis corporate communications to the sudden departure of a critical employee from a high-profile project. Using my back-up planning philosophy I've made it through some pretty trying times! I prepared for the unexpected by building strong teams, really understanding their strengths and weaknesses, finding opportunities to help them grow their skills, developing succession plans and generally maintaining a keen level of awareness of my business environment. It's like keeping the generator tuned-up so that it can deliver the power you need in an emergency.

Are you ready for your next business power outage? Scan your environment and evaluate your resources. Prepare for the worst and when the power comes back on, you will be ahead of everyone else. Oh, and take my advice, get a generator for your house too.

~ Sandra Pacey ~

## *Hold My Feet To The Fire*

Irecently had a discussion about accountability with one of my favorite clients. This company is a leader in their field. They're good at what they do and their confidence shows. They set big goals for themselves and they've made great strides towards meeting them. But they could be doing even better.

Why aren't they? Because when they deliver good results, but not the great ones to which they aspire, they let themselves off the hook. They haven't been holding themselves truly accountable for meeting their audacious targets.

The leadership team has been working together for a number of years. They're nice guys. They work well together, and I'm pretty sure that they consider themselves friends. That's the challenge; how do you hold your friends and colleagues accountable for results? A good approach is to avoid making it personal by using metrics to keep everyone on track.

Accountability requires measurability. As a management team you need to have a process for measuring and reporting progress towards your targets. That way, when the numbers come up short, you can have an objective discussion about what you're going to do about it (then hold each other accountable for the outcomes of those corrective actions!). This principle applies to you as an individual and to your direct reports – in fact it applies right across the organization.

When performance against an objective is measured, and you are holding someone accountable for the results, you must also empower them with the means to succeed. So, along with setting targets, and implementing a measurement and reporting process, you need quality resource planning. Giving someone the resources to get the job done is what cements their commitment to the results and gives you the right to hold them accountable.

I don't want to be too hard on my client. They've already taken steps to develop a culture of accountability. The reason I've thought about this issue so much is that we face it ourselves at Stratford Managers. All through your career you hope to find the kind of people you really want to work with. It is ironic that the respect and friendship that develops between the members of your "dream team" can actually impede your mutual success if you're not careful.

It is so easy to just cut each other some slack. But holding each other accountable for the type of success you know you can achieve together is actually a sign of respect. Treat each other like big boys and girls. Measure your progress, provide adequate resources and make sure you prompt each other to take real action to get those big results. I'd rather have a respected colleague hold my feet to the fire than let me off the hook. That's how I know what they really think of me.

~ Doug Michaelides ~

## *Being On Display*

My recent blog post on accountability, 'Hold My Feet to the Fire', touched a nerve. I had at least half a dozen people sheepishly ask whether I had been talking about them and their company. Interestingly, everyone who contacted me is what I consider to be a high performance manager. In other words, it was the best people that were the most sensitive to the issue of accountability and most concerned about whether they and their teams measured up.

Why would individuals that consistently deliver the goods and inspire others to do the same, be most concerned? It's because good leaders are introspective – they constantly worry about having a blind spot. They know that the best way to lead is by example and that their behavior is on display at all times. Their staff watches them closely for cues on how to act – and they want to ensure that they are living up to their own high expectations. No wonder good leaders are sensitive – it's an enormous responsibility!

Whether we're talking about accountability, customer-focus or teamwork, if a leader isn't "walking the talk", they won't get the desired results from their organization. This doesn't just apply to the CEO, by the way. We all provide leadership to our staff and colleagues in one way or another so we must all monitor our behavior to ensure that it is exemplary. It takes real discipline.

So, if you were squirming a little after reading my last blog post, it's a good sign. I probably wasn't talking about you, but there's no harm wondering. . .

~ Doug Michaelides ~

"LOOK! A BIRD!"

## *Integrity*

What would you do if, while browsing a hated competitor's website, you suddenly found yourself able to access confidential information like customer lists, management reports and internal presentations?

That's the question that presented itself to a young employee of one Stratford Managers client recently. This individual is highly competitive. As is the case for many people in business, the challenge of beating the competition really motivates him to put that extra effort into his work. The competition is "the enemy" and any opportunity to stick it to them is something to relish.

In a world in which the Internet serves up every sort of content at the click of a mouse, the distinction between "public" information and "private" information has blurred. The widespread use of file-sharing sites to freely access copyright-protected content has conditioned many people, especially young people, to regard anything available on the web as fair game for downloading.

This attitude, when carried over to the business function of competitive intelligence, risks having over-enthusiastic employees crossing the line from legitimate data gathering to hacking. It isn't much different from other shady competitive intelligence techniques like hiring a consultant to pose as a customer (recently an Ottawa-based company was accused of posing as a prospective customer in order to gain proprietary information about a competitor in the HR technology industry).

Many companies make a point of promoting corporate integrity. Presumably that means living up to your commitments and not engaging in ethically questionable practices. Corporate policies and, more importantly, the example set by senior managers in an organization all contribute to ensuring that employees act appropriately in their work. However it all starts with personal integrity; with individuals having a clear sense of right and wrong guiding their behavior in an increasingly complex workplace. Character is about what you do when you're alone.

So it is heartening that when this young employee was alone, he resisted temptation and did the right thing. He backed out of the website without looking at confidential documents and immediately advised his management of the situation. The CEO sent an email to his counterpart warning of the security flaw.

Then everyone went back to competing furiously for business, integrity firmly intact.

~ Doug Michaelides ~

## *Celebrating Success With A Personal Touch*

It's the time of year when many of us look back to evaluate our performance. Did we achieve what we set out to achieve? Are we satisfied with our results? Were we successful this year?

Success (whatever that means to you and your company) is a much sought after prize. Plenty of careful strategy, planning and delivery go into our achievements, especially when we set the bar high. A lot of physical, mental and emotional effort is expended. So when that goal is met, what happens next?

Let's say a company has focused heavily on growing revenues and has achieved year end performance that beats even its highest estimates. Many CEOs will send out an email to all staff announcing the good news, thanking the team and exhorting them to continue their efforts into the next fiscal year. Everyone in the company may even receive some sort of commemorative trinket (how many coffee mugs, beer steins and T-shirts have you accumulated over the years?) Yet emails get deleted and trinkets gather dust in drawers and neither has lasting meaning. These well-intentioned but impersonal ways to recognize success don't properly acknowledge employee contribution or take advantage of the significant opportunity to reinforce a culture of success.

A great company acts differently. Management realizes that people are their biggest asset. Staff who can achieve great results this year will reach even higher performance next year with the right recognition and nurturing. Celebrating success for this type of organization means not only allocating budget to celebrate, but most importantly, allocating time from the executive staff to ensure that their employees are recognized for their part in the company's results.

True leaders will personally thank each of their staff members, taking the time to pull examples from the past year that illustrate their contribution. This personal touch is rocket fuel for staff motivation, creating a desire to do even better next year. Even a simple "thank-you" with a warm handshake from a respected manager can be enough to reward and motivate your staff. Best of all, a company party where people celebrate their shared success with their colleagues, including the executive staff, is an excellent way to cap a good year and build momentum for the next! If a commemorative coffee mug is handed out too, well, now it means something.

The moral of the story is to never miss an opportunity to celebrate your successes. Celebrations are appreciated and remembered; it's part of the human psyche. Over time, these celebrations become part of your company's "story" and shared history. When you hit or exceed your targets, celebrate big (and personally) so your staff will be re-charged and ready to conquer the next hill! Sustaining this momentum into a culture of success is what differentiates the great companies from the rest!

~ Joe Connelly ~

## What Were You Expecting?

In a now-famous experiment conducted during the '64-'65 school year, researchers gave teachers at Oak School a list of student names. They told the teachers that these students had scored in the top 10% of their class in a new, specialized test that measured intellectual capacity and predicted learning "spurts".

In fact, the researchers had given a generic IQ test and had chosen the names on the list randomly, not based on the test scores. At the end of the school year, the researchers gave the students the IQ test again and looked for any correlation between the results and the names on the original list. Guess what they found?

The IQ score improvements for students on the list were 50% higher than for the rest of the class! Astoundingly, just because the teachers expected certain randomly selected kids to learn faster – they actually did. This is called the Expectation Effect and has been demonstrated in numerous similar studies.

In business, we often expect certain outcomes without realizing that our expectations are in fact influencing the results. There is a management maxim that says, "you get what you measure." Let me also suggest that "you get what you expect."

One of our clients asked us to help find ways to improve their profitability. We concluded that they should increase prices. They objected, "Our customers won't pay more. We often lose business to our competitors because of price." Yet, some of their competitors were charging higher prices and getting higher profits.

I think we were seeing the Expectation Effect. Our client expected that their customers wouldn't tolerate higher prices. This belief prevented them from thinking about what they needed to do in order to successfully charge higher prices. Do you see the subtle but powerful force at play? Our client had fallen victim to a self-fulfilling prophecy without even realizing it.

We see this happening in many businesses. Here are some ideas for avoiding this trap:

1. Spend some time benchmarking your competitors. Search for examples of the Expectation Effect in your company by looking at yourself through their eyes.
2. Meet regularly with an independent board of directors or advisors that can challenge your assumptions and help expose the Expectation Effect.
3. Write down your key targets to make your expectations explicit. Then question them.
4. Hire people who by their nature challenge the status quo. Listen to them.
5. Get in the habit of asking "Why?" or "Why not?" This is a powerful way to expose assumptions.

Growing a profitable company requires many skills. You have to get a lot of things right. Ironically, the biggest risk may be in the way you think about your business and in the expectations you have for it. So, beware the Expectation Effect and remember the new maxim "you get what you expect."

~ Jim Roche ~

## *Striving for Clarity*

Eric and Stephanie are getting married. They met at a dance, dated for a while and then made the big decision. They even decided to live together before the wedding. Essentially, they collected data about each other and then committed. Are they certain that their future together will be happy until "death do us part"? Of course not! There's no way to be certain. However, they believe that they will be happy and they are clear about their commitment.

Most business decisions of any significance are just like that. You need some data to make the decision. You might try an idea out for size by modeling it or running a pilot project. But if you wait for enough data to be certain that you're making the right decision, you'll never act.

Tough decisions are about the future and the future is never certain. Should I hire this person? Should I invest in this new product? Should I sign this contract? Expand in this market? Acquire this company? Let this company acquire mine? Start a business? End a business? These are all tough decisions.

Get some data. Try the decision on for size if you can. But forget about certainty; strive instead for clarity.

Eric and Stephanie could have lived together for years before committing to marriage. But they didn't. They learned about each other, tried the decision on for size and made a commitment. They are clear.

Congratulations to them both.

~ Jim Roche ~

# III.
# Marketing

## *Tradeshow Skeptic*

Over the years, I've become a bit of a tradeshow skeptic. Events are expensive and the results are often hard to measure. Plus I hate the subtle threats cloaked in the pitches of tradeshow organizers who are more interested in their business than mine.

In the old days tradeshows were one of the best ways to reach a target market. The event organizers promised to do the work of bringing in the right audience so all you had to do was show up and make a good impression. These days, there are so many other ways to reach a target market that the ROI for events must be weighed against alternatives like webinars, email marketing, social media, etc.

Yet the one thing I've always liked about events is that they come with a deadline. The rush to prepare creates a massive spike in marketing productivity. Marketing messages are developed. Press releases are written. Collateral is prepared. Websites are updated. Special promotions are created. There is nothing like an event to galvanize a product launch or an entry into a new market!

Unfortunately, the excitement of events can be addictive. There is always someone – a channel partner, a sales rep, a product manager or an executive – who wants to do a show. It is all too easy for a zombie marketing department to stagger from show to show, driving up costs and reducing marketing ROI. So the trick is to use this marketing tool sparingly.

To keep things under control, use metrics to encourage dispassionate decision-making. Depending on the objectives for an event, appropriate metrics may include: media coverage, booth visitors/registrations, client meetings, leads gathered and orders taken. Set targets beforehand, make sure on-site staff are tracking the metrics, and retain the data for benchmarking in the future. And don't forget to track all costs associated with the event (including staff travel and living) so you'll be able to calculate ROI.

Two major corporate "anchor" shows a year is plenty for a mid-sized B2B company. Perhaps add a few smaller niche events, driven by regional priorities. In all cases, plan things up to a year in advance if you want to secure speaking slots, sponsorships or a primo booth location. Most importantly, no event should be undertaken without a comprehensive pre/post-event marketing and lead-nurturing plan. If your events aren't creating a frenzy of marketing activity that delivers results long after the booth is torn down, then this marketing skeptic says save your budget for something more useful.

~ Doug Michaelides ~

## *10 Ways To Build A Fortress (Marketing) Balance Sheet*

Many corporate CFOs have spent the past couple of years preparing their companies for tough economic times by creating "fortress" balance sheets. According to Moody's Investor Services, US public companies have hoarded a staggering $1.5 trillion in cash. But have CMOs built "fortress" <u>marketing</u> balance sheets? Here are 10 things your CMO should have been doing in anticipation of tougher times:

1. Building the brand (awareness and reputation)
2. Improving channel effectiveness and loyalty
3. Implementing strategic account and customer loyalty programs
4. Creating a strong community (based on a strong social media presence)
5. Nurturing relationships with media and analysts
6. Establishing a bullet-proof lead management process (including a CRM and Marketing Automation)
7. Improving the website (design, SEO, registration and conversion capabilities, etc.)
8. Updating sales tools including the collateral suite
9. Developing the competency of marketing staff and recruiting quality vendors
10. Justifying and obtaining a stable budget to sustain marketing programs

It's quite a list, isn't it? Nobody said a CMO's job is easy (except maybe the CFO!). To determine if your marketing balance sheet is sound, consider the following metrics:

- New customer growth
- Customer retention/renewal
- Cross-sell ratio (breadth of portfolio sold to customers)
- Share of wallet (share of customer spending)
- Revenue and margin per channel partner
- Customer satisfaction and channel satisfaction
- Funnel performance: lead value, aging and conversion rates
- Brand awareness
- Website traffic, site ranking and keyword rankings

A strong marketing balance sheet is just as important as the financial one when it comes to preparing for tough times. Like a good investor, you want to avoid being forced to make a snap decision during a crisis. Review your current marketing mix so that when the inevitable belt-tightening comes, you know what's expendable.

Market leaders reap the benefits of strong balance sheets by staying engaged with the market and using times of uncertainty to pull ahead of their competition. So, by all means, build a marketing "fortress" but for goodness sake don't raise the drawbridge, hide in your tower and wait for the barbarians to retreat!

~ Doug Michaelides ~

## *Lead Management That Suits*

There I was, in my snazzy new suit, talking about how to structure a lead management system. I was about to sketch a funnel to illustrate the stages of an interconnected marketing and sales lead process. Reaching into my inside suit jacket pocket, I fished out my pen when a small square of green paper fluttered onto the table.

My client raised a quizzical eyebrow as I unfolded the paper, like a fortune cookie message, to read the printing: "#20 – Final Examination". I realized that it was a tag placed in the suit pocket at the final quality inspection. Searching my suit pockets I discovered other slips of paper: "#3 – Creasing" and "#8 – Finished Press". Going with the flow, I asked my client, " If it takes 20 steps to finish a suit, how many do you think it takes to manage a lead?"

Together we laid out an integrated marketing and sales funnel that started like this:

**Marketing Funnel:** 1. Contacts (email list, webinar audience, etc.), 2. Suspects, 3. Prospects, 4. Opportunities.

I stressed the importance of being clear about the criteria used to promote a lead from one stage of the funnel to the next, and about who would be responsible for managing and reporting on the leads at each stage. Grey areas in the lead management process are the enemy of conversion rates!

We defined the lead-scoring criteria (e.g. website activity, company name and title, pre-qualification by Inside Sales, etc.) for each level. At the "opportunity" stage a lead became sufficiently qualified to pass from the marketing funnel to the sales funnel with the next steps:

**Sales Funnel:** 4. Opportunities, 5. Proposals, 6. Revenues

We agreed with the VP of Sales that once a lead became an "opportunity", it would be assigned a provisional dollar value, a probability of closure and a timeline so that it could become part of the sales forecast. New leads resulting from executive business development and referrals could be injected at the appropriate stage in the funnel then added to the opportunities.

Then we selected metrics to track so that the company would have visibility on future revenues based on the state of the funnel. Fortunately we had some historic data on conversion rates (% of leads that progressed from one stage to the next), lead aging at each stage and typical deal sizes so we could benchmark performance. We would use the existing CRM system for the sales funnel but, until we implemented a Marketing Automation System, the marketing funnel would be managed with spreadsheets.

After about an hour's work, my client pushed back his chair from the conference room table and said proudly, "Doug, I think we've just tailored a process that fits my business like . . . a custom-made designer suit!" I smiled, pleased but knowing that there'd still some alterations before I'd be ready to put my name on the label!

~ Doug Michaelides ~

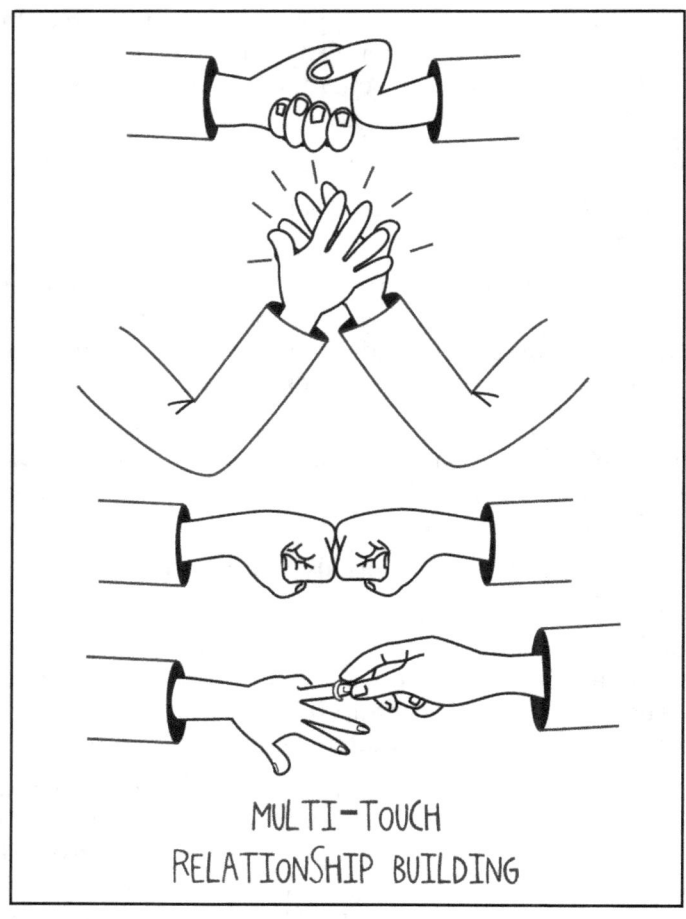

MULTI-TOUCH
RELATIONSHIP BUILDING

# The Nurturing Type

I often see energetic marketers pour their hearts into stand-alone marketing initiatives. They brag about their leads, and then they restlessly move on to their next infatuation.

The difference between amateur marketers and professionals is that the professionals are in it for a long time, not just a good time. Each of their marketing initiatives incorporates a call to action. Every call to action leads to another interaction that is the next step along the path of nurturing a relationship. The amateurs are scoring one-night stands. The professionals are cultivating serious romances.

It takes time for a marketing team to develop the maturity and discipline required for effective lead nurturing. The complexity involved in setting up a multi-touch marketing program that employs a variety of materials and executes over several months is enough to give anyone cold feet! Yet that's what it takes to progress from ad hoc (and often unreliable) lead generation to sustained demand creation.

The good news is that there are a number of ways of making multi-touch demand creation programs easier. Here are some key elements:

1. A website that can be easily modified to add content and create landing pages
2. Registration/opt-in capability (either built into the website or using a marketing automation system – see item 6)
3. A customer relationship management (CRM) system for sales people to manage leads to closure
4. Quality content (keep in mind that content can and should be frequently re-used. Your core marketing campaigns should cycle through standard content that reflects your unique value proposition and offering – which don't change that often)
5. Multi-channel outbound communications (email, social media, traditional media, advertising, etc.)
6. A marketing automation system (a good one will enable you to manage your contact database, send emails, establish landing pages, track and score leads, promote leads to the CRM, map out the elements of multi-touch campaigns and provide reports)

But all the sexy marketing tools in the world aren't enough. You have to have the will to change your wanton ways. So, young marketer, now that you've had your fill of marketing hook-ups, it is time to settle down and commit to longer-term, multi-touch relationship-building programs. Do this and you'll lose your reputation for fickle marketing and become widely admired as the nurturing type.

~ Doug Michaelides ~

## *Golfing for Marketers*

I found myself on the links for the first round of golf of the season a few days ago (actually, it was my first time in 3 years which tells you a whole lot about my game…). Since golf is a thinking person's game, while hunting for my ball I got thinking about the many parallels between golf and marketing.

I started to relate the 18 holes in a golf course to the series of marketing campaigns that a typical company might run over the course of a year. A successful round of golf is the accumulation of many effective strokes just as a good marketing campaign is the sum of several tactics. Each stroke, requiring a different club, is like one of the 3-5 marketing tactics that should be part of a campaign. We "tee-off" with a press release or editorial coverage, play the fairway with social media and blog posts, chip onto the green with a webinar or event, then putt for par with an email blast that brings the prospects back to our e-commerce website or sales team to make the sale.

Serious golfers know that spending money on a good set of clubs will lower their score (as does hiring a pro for lessons now and then). Effective marketing requires money be spent on good marketing tactics too. So ask the CFO, does he want to play golf or go bowling?

Obviously technique is important as well. A small change in your swing can have a big impact on your game. That's why good marketers track metrics and adjust their tactics. Sadly however, in golf, as in marketing, there are many factors that you just can't control. Your swing may be perfect but you can still land in the bunker.

Even in a friendly game, someone is keeping score. So you need to take the time to plan your strategy for every hole and carefully execute each shot, checking your grip, your stance and your swing. But, if you're progressing too slowly, there's always the risk that the marshal will pull you off the course. Many a CMO has spent the summer practicing his swing after not delivering results fast enough for the CEO's liking!

Can you think of other analogies between golfing and marketing? I'm convinced that golf is popular because it's a metaphor for many other things in life. It's frustrating, infuriating and just often enough, when everything comes together, elating. I find I get enough of that excitement doing marketing, which probably explains why I've only golfed once in the past 3 years!

~ Doug Michaelides ~

## *Keep It Simple Smart-Guy*

I work with a lot of smart marketing people who take sophisticated products and services to market. With all this brainpower you'd think that the marketing messages would be clear, concise and highly effective. In fact, often the opposite is true.

Smart marketers trying to differentiate their products and services too often resort to increasingly nuanced messages. They struggle to squeeze the last drop of value proposition from their offer and strive to own the smallest whitespace in the competitive landscape. The result is that value propositions and communications campaigns end up with the complexity of fine wine. Unfortunately, a thirsty market mostly just wants water.

When your value propositions are complex you are narrowing your potential audience. You are probably also obscuring the most important elements of your offer in a haze of related, but initially less important, detail. Marketing communications become harder, the sales team can't articulate the message and, in general, prospective customers don't get it. Here's a sign; if your sales and executive teams are complaining that the corporate message is unclear (if everyone's avoiding the elevator because they don't know the pitch), then odds are you're trying to make it too complex.

That good first impression with prospective customers is going to be made not by subtle statements of differentiated value but by a strong core value proposition that hits their concerns head on. Don't worry if the core value proposition isn't all that strongly differentiated – your primary objective up front is to catch the attention of prospective buyers. Once interested they'll spend more time with you to learn the many ways you're unique, through subsequent marketing and sales interactions.

Buyers are looking for choice. It is a wide world out there, with lots of room for companies who, on the surface, appear to offer similar value propositions. So unless you're up against a dominant, market-defining player (e.g. Cisco in routers, Google in search, Starbucks in coffee) it's often better to worry a little less about differentiating yourself from the competition and more about just getting your company in front of prospective buyers.

So, try to keep it simple smart-guy! Granted, simple isn't easy to do. Samuel Johnson once said, "I did not have time to write you a short letter, so I wrote you a long one instead." You have to work hard to write less and focus on fewer ideas. Hammer on a simple core value proposition that strongly resonates with your target market. Your marketing and sales people (and channel partners) will thank you for making their life easier and you'll have more success filling the top of the funnel.

~ Doug Michaelides ~

## *Do Away With Marketing?*

I spend a lot of my time trying to explain to people why Marketing is important. So it was somewhat disconcerting when a friend of mine exclaimed over lunch, "Maybe we should just do away with Marketing!"

It was going to be a long lunch…

We had been discussing why e-commerce initiatives so often seem to yield poor results. I had been relating a positive experience I'd recently had buying a camera from a really good e-commerce website and was wondering why all e-stores weren't like that. I had concluded that this site must have been designed by marketers who cared about customer experience rather than IT-types who were more interested in ease of implementation.

In fact, my friend didn't have it in for the function of marketing itself, just the artificial barriers we create between groups of people in an organization. Maybe if the marketing people and the IT people working together on an e-commerce project felt like they were part of the same team, with the same objectives, then the outcome would be better.

"What I mean", he continued, "Is that we shouldn't think of Marketing as just a 'department'. Since many people are involved, we should just get them all together and call it something else that's more meaningful."

"How about 'Revenue Enablement'?, I offered. That seemed to work for him.

Then I got thinking. What if you renamed the Sales and Marketing departments in your company "Revenue Enablement"? It might just help align priorities, focus efforts and result in greater cooperation. You see, when you talk about what you deliver (revenue) rather than what you do (marketing and sales) there is a constant reminder of the real purpose of your work.

Think it's kind of a wacky idea? Obviously it mustn't be just lip-service but perhaps the renaming of the function <u>could</u> be a first step towards a better overall go-to-market model. After all, how many organizations do you know that have renamed their "Technical Support" groups "Customer Service"?

~ Doug Michaelides ~

## *Process is Not a Four Letter Word*

I've heard the complaint many times from my marketing communications teams: "There's too much process!" Marcoms people like to be unconstrained so they have the freedom to deliver exceptional creativity, but then reality sets in . . .

A client or senior manager reviews a creative proposal and yelps, "That doesn't work! It needs to be flashier and much cooler than that!" Except, "flashier and cooler" means…what exactly?

What it usually means is that the original creative brief turned into a fun brainstorming session with everyone feeling really good about all the great ideas and happy that they were part of it. Unfortunately, it also means that the creative briefing process broke down. As a marcoms professional you don't ever want that to happen, so here's how to avoid it.

First, do your homework! Marketing communications staff must always come to the briefing meeting prepared. Interview stakeholders, clearly define what differentiates you from the competition and understand what the competitors are doing. Make sure that you have nailed the campaign objectives and the three key messages so you can use the meeting to get buy-in from the stakeholders. Allow the free flow of ideas but ensure that the results are aligned with the key messages. Don't leave the meeting without agreement and follow up with an email confirming the outcome and identifying the next steps.

Next, select the appropriate communication vehicles and message for each audience, whether they are customers, channel members, or partners. Make a schedule of all the activities, from conception through to delivery, to ensure you're not competing for resources or conflicting with other events that your audience may be interested in. Finally, measure where you can – metrics are a key element of the process and ultimately reveal whether the communications strategy has worked.

Proper processes for marketing communications strategy, operations and creation-delivery drive effective behaviors that improve the timeliness and efficiency of your marcoms projects. It's really just employing solid project management principles to your marketing initiatives.

It takes a deft touch for a marketing manager to impose process on the creative members of the marketing communications team. But the effort will bring your products or services to life for your targeted audiences in a reliable and cost-effective manner.

And once you get good at employing just the right amount of process at the right time, it will become so natural for your staff that rather than complaints, you'll probably just hear "You see? We don't really need a whole bunch of process after all!"

~ Sandra Pacey ~

## *Creating Content*

I've written about how budget constraints often undercut the success of sustained marketing campaigns. Another frequent cause is inability to create content. Many a marketer has moaned about the challenge of sourcing sufficient quality content from their organization to produce whitepapers, blog posts, tweets, webinars, presentations, case studies, newsletters, editorial articles, press releases, brochures, datasheets, etc.

The key to sustaining marketing communications campaigns (which we all know is the only way to generate results over time) is to create a rhythm in the creation of content. Why not make this a marketing New Year's resolution? Here are some suggestions how:

- Identify content primes (as many subject matter experts as you can find)
- Create a regular schedule for delivery of content (weekly, monthly, quarterly) and designate someone to follow-up
- Provide them with ideas and examples of the content you desire
- Don't ask for finished product . . . point-form is fine!
- Consider outsourced assistance to help with writing, design and formatting ("I can't write" is the number one reason given by subject matter experts for not creating content)
- Offer to record audio or video interviews if your subject matter experts prefer
- Use interviews – they are great for getting content from reluctant contributors
- Repurpose relentlessly (whitepapers become editorials become newsletters become blog posts and website content)

Valuable content is the marketing "honey" that attracts prospects to your campaigns. With a well-established content creation rhythm, you'll be able to create the kind of "buzz" your company deserves.

And for all you brilliant but reluctant subject matter experts out there, give a marketer a break. Resolve to write a few pieces of content. You may find that you're better at it than you think!

~ Doug Michaelides ~

## *Brilliant Business Models*

Sometimes you learn about a business model whose brilliance just takes your breath away. You shake your head and wonder how anyone ever thought of it.

These days, the most brilliant business models tend to take advantage of the amazing power of the Internet to create micro-markets where none appear to exist. Everyone knows what mass markets are. Those are the ones where a whole bunch of people want the same thing. They are easy to find. Of course, they are easy to find for everyone else too so there is usually a lot of competition.

Micro-markets, on the other hand, are "gaseous" – a relatively small number of people spread out within an enormous volume of market space. Under normal circumstances you'd never be able to find them. And if you can't find them, you can't sell to them. But what if they could find you?

That's the brilliant idea behind two exciting web enterprises called www.kiva.org and www.kickstarter.com

Kiva's mission is to connect people, through lending, to alleviate poverty. It combines charitable microfinance with the Internet to enable individuals like you and me to lend to a poor entrepreneur somewhere across the globe. As a lender, you review the projects on Kiva's website, decide which to finance (you can fully or partially fund an initiative) then watch its progress over time. The entrepreneur uses the funds received from all lenders to operate a small business venture – I lent money to an African woman to help buy a motorcycle for a milk delivery service. Lenders get repaid over time so they can reinvest their charitable funds again and again with other entrepreneurs. Lenders don't make any money but the idea of extending this to for-profit venture funding isn't far-fetched.

A slightly more commercial approach is taken by Kickstarter, the largest funding platform for creative projects in the world. Every month, tens of thousands of people pledge millions of dollars to projects from creative fields like music, film, art, technology, design, food and publishing. In this case, people aren't lending or investing, they are "pre-purchasing" products or experiences offered by project creators. I've pledged to buy a strap from a design firm called MINIMAL that will transform my iPod Nano into a cool multi-touch watch. A project must reach its funding goal before time runs out or no money changes hands. That way, purchasers are protected and creators aren't expected to develop their project without necessary funds. The beauty of Kickstarter's approach is that anyone can test market a concept without financial risk.

In all cases, the low marginal cost of reaching people over the Internet enables markets to coalesce out of thin air by bringing together an extremely diffuse interest group.

*<shakes his head>* Simply brilliant!

~ Doug Michaelides ~

# Dispatches from the Front Lines

Good marketers are obsessed with metrics. We spend a lot of time trying to figure out whom we are reaching and what kind of impact we are having. We use web analytics to track traffic on our websites. We use marketing automation systems to monitor email campaign performance and lead generation. Those of us with money commission brand awareness research. Like satellites overhead we look down on the marketing battlefield to gain the intelligence we need to improve our campaigns. In fact, we are so enamored with our high-tech marketing metrics that sometimes we forget to monitor the old fashion "dispatches from the front lines" that our sales and customer service teams create every day.

Is your marketing team on the distribution list for the following market intelligence?

- Win/Loss Reports (or "Notices of Sales")
- Sales Call Reports
- Customer Service Reports

If you are not monitoring these important sources of information, you're not getting a full picture of the market. Worse still, you risk developing marketing plans that are disconnected from the daily experiences of the sales team.

Not all companies have implemented these reporting practices, but they should. These reports help marketing people monitor the customer experience, watch their value propositions and sales tools in action (or not!), track emerging competitive threats and get early warning of weaknesses in the product that need to be addressed. This is actionable information that is highly relevant to near term revenue and the effectiveness of the sales team. For any marketer, the chance to virtually walk in the shoes of the sales force and customer service team is the best market research you'll ever get . . . and it's free!

Marketers, like general staff in the armed forces, are sometimes accused of being out of touch with the action in the trenches. This is particularly a concern in multi-national businesses. They sit in their ergonomic chairs in their fancy headquarters offices, pouring over their web statistics, oblivious to the real needs of the field. Yet the sales team is sending up flares and calling for air cover all the time. You just need to pay attention. So make sure you open the lines of communication by reading these reports and having a dialogue with the people who write them. Not only will your relationship with the sales team improve, you will gain confidence in your marketing decisions.

After all, in the words of U.S. General George S. Patton, "*No good decision was ever made in a swivel chair.*"

~ Doug Michaelides ~

## *Many Coins Frequently Tossed*

Something that non-marketers have a hard time understanding is that marketing is a non-deterministic endeavor. It is not always possible to connect a particular outcome with a specific initiative. Instead, it is a probabilistic undertaking; every action accumulates to increase the odds of the desired results.

This may sound like there is an element of faith to marketing; I prefer to think of it as building confidence. Flip a single coin one time and you might not get "heads". Flip multiple coins at the same time, or a single coin multiple times, and you are confident that you will.

That's why marketers like to run sustained, integrated marketing campaigns. Integrated marketing means using a variety of different, complementary methods to achieve your objective. For example, to raise awareness, you advertise plus participate in tradeshows plus issue press releases plus execute viral campaigns. Like tossing a single coin, an individual awareness initiative may not give you the result you want, but the weight of the combined efforts (flipping several coins) increases the odds of success. Sustaining these efforts over time (multiple flips of the coins) gives you even greater confidence of a positive outcome.

Now let's talk about spending coin. . .

Effective marketing requires spending enough to run integrated campaigns on a sustained basis. It is the great tragedy of marketing that the marketing budget is often the first one to be sacrificed when financial targets are under pressure. As the elements of an integrated marketing plan are whittled away and the campaigns are pared back or shortened, the odds of success decrease. Unsatisfactory results from eviscerated marketing campaigns then confirm the thinking that led to the cuts in the first place.

Successful companies have the confidence in marketing, and their marketing teams, to adequately fund integrated campaigns and sustain the spending so it has a chance to yield results. They don't gamble on a single toss of a coin.

~ Doug Michaelides ~

## *Re-Tooling for E-Commerce*

The world of commerce continues to move on-line. Amazon.com is now selling more eBooks than hard covers (a lot more). ITunes and similar services have replaced the bricks and mortar music store. And with Netflix offering its on-line streaming video service in Canada. you can kiss Rogers Video and Blockbuster goodbye! Businesses just can't ignore e-commerce as a new channel to market, even for B2B products/services. To take advantage of the increasing willingness to buy on-line, companies need to consider a number of things:

1.  Is your website up to the task? Obviously you need a robust e-commerce engine (shopping carts, etc.) but a website originally designed as an on-line corporate brochure isn't that great for generating leads let alone guiding visitors through the entire buying process.
2.  Is your product priced for on-line purchase? There is still a limit to the price point people are willing to pay on-line with a credit card, even for business purposes (though it may be quite a bit higher than you imagine). You can stretch this amount through trials, demos and previews.
3.  Have you thought about using a "Freemium" pricing strategy? (not everyone agrees with this premise, by the way, including Malcolm Gladwell)
4.  What is your sustained marketing plan to get prospective buyers to your e-commerce site? You can't rely just on SEO. Can you create an on-line community around your products?
5.  Does there need to be a lead management process to hand-off higher-value, more complex opportunities to traditional sales channels?
6.  How will you secure ongoing revenue streams (create customers that will return and buy again)?
7.  Do you have a Business Intelligence process? I mean not only keeping records of your "tryers" and "buyers" for ongoing nurturing and upgrades, but also analyzing the navigation and abandonment patterns in your website to improve purchasing rates. Seemingly subtle improvements to your website navigation and layout can make a big difference.
8.  Have you considered the possible conflict with your current channels to market? You don't want to undercut your loyal channel partners or sales reps (unless you plan to drop them). How will e-commerce sales be considered for quota retirement and commission purposes?
9.  How will you handle after-sales support? User community supported? On-line self-service? Telephone/email support? Field support?

Just because everyone seems to be doing it, doesn't mean it is easy to do well. Implementing a successful e-commerce strategy is a significant undertaking, particularly for a business that has traditionally relied on personal selling. It demands a major retooling of many aspects of your marketing, sales and product strategy. However, implemented correctly e-commerce can deliver that holy grail of business; earning you money while you sleep!

~ Doug Michaelides ~

## *Fish Where the Fishes Are*

I have a cottage.

Something most people who know me don't know about me is that I love to go fishing. I enjoy the solitude, the time to think, the mixture of luck and skill plus the satisfaction of being smarter than a fish (sometimes). Fishing also teaches life lessons. It rewards patience, getting up early, imagination, and wearing a hat in the sun.

The key to a successful fishing trip (as measured by size of catch) is to fish where the fishes are. It's the same for successful marketing (especially if you're a smaller business without a well-established brand).

A big brand name is like a light shone into dark waters. It attracts fish that can then be caught. Those of us without the bright light of a well-known brand can't count on our prospects coming to us so, instead, we need to go where they gather. That's why many marketers like tradeshows.

Web marketers and social media types talk about communities (Seth Godin uses the term "tribes"). If you can find out where your communities of interest hang out, then you can target your marketing efforts (gently) towards these places. This will deliver better marketing return on investment vs. a shotgun approach. It also gives you the chance to co-opt your audience to help promote your products.

Think about your bait when you go fishing this way (whitepapers, blog posts, video, webinars, etc.). You need to provide value to get the attention of your community, particularly if you are trying to get a prospect to take an action (e.g. subscribe to a newsletter/blog, etc.).

You do have a call to action don't you? This is the equivalent of setting the hook so you can reel them in over time (don't reel too fast or play around too much otherwise you risk losing them).

Finally, ensure that there is a sales person or e-commerce capability around with a net to land your catch!

Happy fishing!

~ Doug Michaelides ~

## Marketing and Sales Performance? Check!

Checklists are a common tool used by professionals to help manage complex tasks. Surgical staff in operating rooms use checklists to reduce the chance of errors during complex operations. Pilots use them during takeoffs, landings and emergencies so that no vital step is missed during these intense activities. In fact, some commentators credit the use of an emergency landing procedures checklist with the successful landing of US Airways Flight 1549 on the Hudson River after both engines failed. Why then aren't checklists more widely used in the complex world of business?

Like flying a plane, running an effective marketing or sales function is a complex, time-sensitive endeavor that can have a critical impact on corporate financial results. At Stratford Managers, we use performance checklists with our clients to help them identify areas for improvement in their business operations. In the marketing department, the checklist covers 17 leadership dimensions within seven major categories of activities: Product, Price, Promotion, Place (familiar so far?), Planning, Process and People. On the Sales side there are four major categories with a total of 12 leadership dimensions. Each category contains several areas that we ask our clients to consider when assessing their performance.

It is a highly useful exercise, especially for senior executives like CEOs who may not be expert in a specific field like marketing or sales. The value isn't just in the assessment of performance in each dimension; it is also in the demonstration of the complexity and inter-relatedness of the various areas of activity. A good checklist encourages understanding and cooperation between the various functions in an organization.

We see many reactions to the idea of using a checklist as a diagnostic tool. For some, it takes the magic out of the function by breaking it down into discrete elements. For others, it is embarrassing or threatening to have their area of responsibility dissected and evaluated in detail. But once managers realize that a checklist is simply a tool to assist them in understanding a complex business function so they can improve performance, their enthusiasm grows.

Rather than flying by the seat of their pants, the best pilots get that way precisely because they use checklists to ensure top performance every time they enter the flight deck.

~ Doug Michaelides ~

THE MARKETING TEAM

# *How Many P's in Marketing?*

Just about everyone knows about the 4 P's of Marketing. Heck, being able to recite the 4 elements of the marketing mix is halfway to having an MBA! (in case you're in need of a refresher, that's: Product, Price, Promotion and….Place, meaning distribution or how you sell your product). But just like everything else these days, there has been inflation in the P's of Marketing.

Pundits add at least two, sometimes three more P's to the list, along the way changing the scope to include not just the "marketing mix" but also other elements in the marketing domain. Some examples:

- Planning (alignment between marketing and corporate strategy)
- Process (business intelligence, lead management, etc.)
- People (resource levels, skill sets, leadership, etc.)

So, depending on who you're talking to, you might have anywhere from 4 to 7 P's in Marketing. I personally like to include the extra P's when I'm working with clients to assess the performance (gulp . . . another P) of their marketing functions. Building a checklist or scorecard around these performance dimensions really helps focus the mind on areas for improvement.

It's important to recognize that when it comes to Planning, Process and People (as well as some of the traditional P's), the responsibility for effectiveness rests not just with the marketing department but also with the entire senior management team. Loose corporate planning, poor IT infrastructure or weak HR practices all have an enormous impact on the effectiveness of marketing activities.

~ Doug Michaelides ~

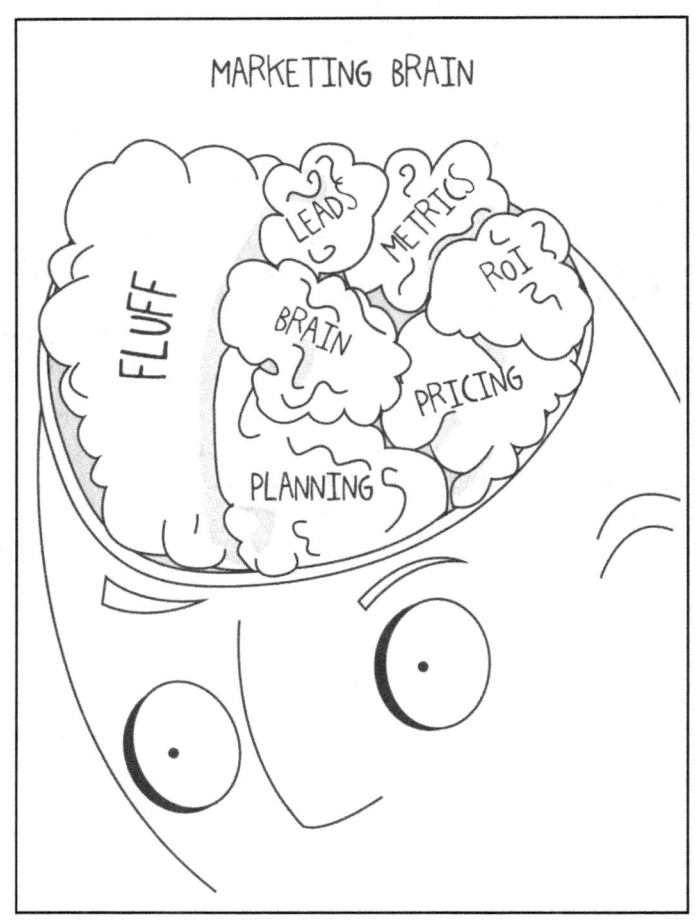

## *Pragmatic Marketing*

Early in my career, after earning a degree in Engineering, I got an MBA and went into Marketing. I've come to realize that my early Engineering training now informs the "pragmatic" approach I take to marketing.

Wiktionary defines pragmatism as: "the pursuit of practicality over aesthetic qualities; a concentration on facts rather than emotions or ideals." The thing that drives hard-nosed financial and technical executives nuts about marketing is the perceived focus on "fluffy" matters like brand, social media and "customer experience". These things are frustratingly hard to connect to concrete results like revenues and marketers don't do themselves any favors by using squishy MBA-speak when explaining what they do.

So, here's my take on the essential elements of pragmatic marketing:

1.  Have a process for **planning** that draws upon multiple sources and engages the entire marketing team. Publish a marketing **calendar** linked to revenue targets, sales activities and new product introductions.
2.  While marketing execution may be about emotion (we want the market to develop an emotional connection with our brand), the rationale for marketing initiatives must be **ROI**.
3.  Marketing spending must be "hard-working". Spend on brand awareness, but make sure you're **generating leads** from the same campaigns. Have a clear call to action and measure the response.
4.  Measure and report results. If you can't measure the outcome of your initiatives, are you leading with your head or your gut? No marketing initiative is complete without a plan for tracking **metrics**.
5.  Protect your **pricing**. Marketers sometimes forget that their role isn't just to generate awareness and leads. They also have a responsibility for maintaining price levels and margins.
6.  Really **listen** to your sales team and channel partners. Sure, they are self-serving at times but they know what is needed to grow revenues. Make sure that you, in turn, are providing high-quality, quantitative **feedback** to your product team.
7.  Act like you own the company. Manage your **budget** and earn a reputation for fiscal responsibility. A CFO that trusts you will be more open to marketing investment.

Marketing is both an art and science. Pragmatic marketing is the science side of things. It's also hard work. The pay-off is better results as well as the respect and support of your colleagues in other functional roles.

~ Doug Michaelides ~

## Marketing the Marketing

Marketing is sometimes the Rodney Dangerfield of corporate functions (it gets "no respect"). Part of this relates to the topic of a previous post ("<u>Pragmatic Marketing</u>") in which I suggested that marketers need to put more effort into quantifying ROI and tracking performance metrics. But, ironically, part of the problem relates to a lack of….marketing!

It's a case of the cobbler's children going without shoes. Marketing people are often too busy concentrating on the market to find the time to speak to their own stakeholders. This is understandable but nonetheless a problem for a couple of reasons.

First, as all good marketers (should) know, a brand is built from the inside out. A brand is a "promise" being made to the consumer and a company's employees must deliver on this promise. So, it is essential for the health (and truth) of the corporate brand that the marketing department enables employees to live the brand. As the custodians of the brand, it is up to marketers to facilitate employee connection to that brand through internal marketing. Any marketer that is leaving all internal communications to the HR department is not providing the kind of leadership their company needs.

Second, in order to sustain investment in marketing initiatives, marketers must ensure that corporate decision-makers (those who control the purse strings) are aware of the impact that they having on the health of the company. This means making commitments (in terms of brand awareness, lead generation, channel development, product introduction, etc.), establishing metrics and reporting progress. The organization must be shown the return on investment from marketing activities if you expect that investment to continue. It also helps if you do your reporting with some flair. Remember, you do have a reputation to maintain and the medium is part of the message. One person's monthly activity report is another's internal marketing campaign.

Marketing the marketing can be motivational not just for marketing staff (everyone likes to show off their work) but also for the entire company, including the executive team. It feeds the corporate ego and, provided your marketing is based on reality, reinforces success.

So, when was the last time you got on your soapbox and put some effort into internal communications?

~ Doug Michaelides ~

## *Launching a Website*

Ilove building websites because it combines the core aspects of marketing: understanding your target audience, being clear on your value proposition, creating an engaging brand image and generating demand.

**Target audience**: which "personas" are your website meant to talk to? Until you know whom you're trying to talk to on your website, you can't decide what outcome you want from the conversation or what you should be saying. Companies used to talking about just product features must change their approach by focusing on the motivation of their target audience instead.

**Value Proposition**: Your value proposition is about what problem you solve (ideally better than any other solution available). This sounds trivial but if you ask 10 people in your company to articulate your value proposition, you'll probably get half a dozen different answers. You need to sift through all this and isolate the core value proposition. The home page of your website should be devoted to this core value.

**Brand Image**: Even hard-nosed business executives who dismiss branding in their own companies readily respond to well managed brand images like Nike, Apple, IBM, Google, Wayne Gretzky, Tiger Woods (oops!), etc. Even if your audience weren't able to read your website copy, they should have a sense of your company's value (and values) from the visual design cues. So, when your marketing team agonizes over colors, layout, fonts, etc., they are not just fooling around. They are trying to communicate your value proposition in a subliminal language that reinforces the words you use.

**Generating Demand**: Think of website visitors as people wandering into a retail store. How do you convert their interest into revenue? A website can take your visitors through all the stages of the buying process from need recognition, information search, evaluation of alternatives, to purchase decision (via e-commerce) and even post-purchase behavior. For more complex business-to-business products/services, a website can create leads for personal selling to convert. So, your website must be integrated into a sound lead management process for nurturing and closing opportunities.

The value of developing an effective website isn't just in the resulting pages on the web. It is in the deep thought that should go into preparing the content and developing the supporting processes. At the end of the exercise, your value proposition should be clear, your target market well defined and your lead management process in place. And because the development of a website is a consultative process, you will have created consensus within the company on these topics.

Clearly a big website project is too important to leave to a designer, web developer or a marketing communications team. No offense meant to any of these important functions but the website needs to be the responsibility of the senior marketing executive and must have the attention of the whole management team.

~ Doug Michaelides ~

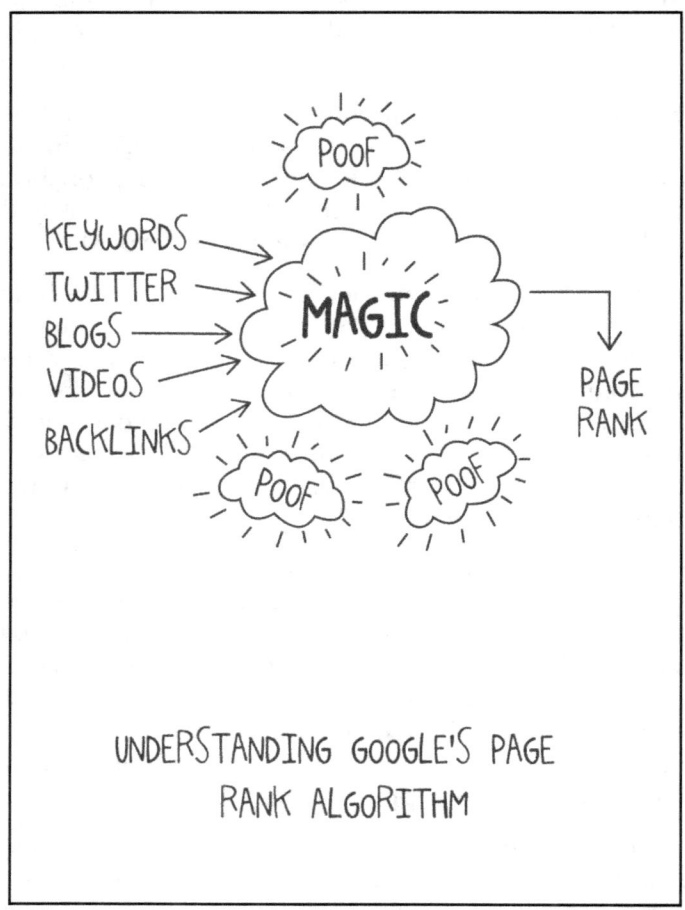

UNDERSTANDING GOOGLE'S PAGE
RANK ALGORITHM

## *Web Marketing Through the Eyes of a Salesman*

Marketers use web sites to promote their company to potential clients. When it works, the sales team enjoys receiving leads. Everyone is happy until … suddenly you're way down the search engine results page. Or worse, you're several pages behind your competition. Why? It's because Google continually changes their search algorithms and how they show search results. SEO techniques that once worked don't have the same impact and as more information is shown for each search result, the quantity of entries on the coveted first page has decreased. Google is also more heavily weighting social media (reviews, blogs, tweets, forums, followers, etc.) in determining page ranking.

So here are some suggestions to put you back into the limelight:

- Blog at least once a week with useful content. Remember, just 'cause you're blogging doesn't mean that anyone is reading! You need to promote it.
- Key words and phrases are important. Make sure you also incorporate them into your blogs posts.
- Twitter is a great way to generate a social media following. Try to tweet at least once a day with useful content (observations on industry trends, links to your blog posts, etc.)
- Claim and update your Google Places Page. As Google competes with providers of local buying services (Groupon, Yelp, etc.) this becomes more important, particularly in your local market.
- Optimize your website for mobile viewing. A growing share of searches are done on mobile devices.
- Ask customers to post reviews of your products on popular review sites.
- Remember the power of video. YouTube is now a Google company and the #2 search engine. Video will help your search scores
- You already have a LinkedIn page for your company, right? Create a Facebook page too. Add a 'Like' button and plan on multiple posts per week.

We're experiencing a shift from traditional outbound marketing in which Marketing and Sales try to find customers, to an inbound model in which we help potential clients find us. Take it from an old Sales hand; if Marketing gets these self-qualified visitors in the on-line door, we'll close more business!

~ Kurt Weber ~

## *Whose Life Are You Changing?*

The other day I received the second in a series of rather melodramatic LinkedIn updates from one of my contacts. The storyline went like this:

June 21: *Today marks the end of an era... I have had a blackberry since September 2001. RIP Curve. Long live my white iphone!!!*

June 30: *had a blackberry for 10 yrs. iPhone for a week. Just kinda figured out the bb changed how we work. #iPhone changes how we live.*

What interested me about these tweets wasn't the relative merits of two smartphones, or the angst of changing brand loyalty, but rather what they said about product strategy. They reminded me that underpinning all great products is a compelling core value proposition directed at a target market.

The Blackberry was developed for business use. By enabling access to email while away from the computer, it changed the way people worked. Having a Blackberry quickly became a working-person's status symbol, then an indispensible business tool. The demand for the product exploded among companies of all sizes and RIM made a fortune.

The iPhone was developed for personal use. By combining music, messaging, games and other apps with a mobile phone, it changed the way everyone from kids to seniors spent their time communicating, accessing entertainment and sharing information. It became a status symbol for everyone and is now as common as the wristwatch used to be. Apple has made an even greater fortune.

What's amazing about these two products is how well they address the needs and desires of their target market. Very few product managers get to bring a product like the Blackberry or iPhone to market, but all product managers must have a clear understanding of the target market (is it big enough?) and customer value proposition (is it strong enough?) of their own products. If this actually happened, marketers and sales people wouldn't spend so much time struggling to explain the value of quirky products to ephemeral prospective buyers.

So, explain to me, who's life are you changing with your product? If you figure this out before you actually develop the product, odds are you'll have a better chance of creating something desirable and taking it to market successfully. Then you might make your fortune too!

PS. The iPhone is so ubiquitous that it seems like it has been around forever. In reality, the end of June 2011 marked just the fourth anniversary of its introduction.

~ Doug Michaelides ~

# IV.
## Sales

## *I'm Writing to Inform You of a Price Increase*

Most sales people dread telling customers about a price increase. Along with cold calling, it is perceived as one of the toughest jobs faced by a sales person. It's believed to be fraught with danger, potentially causing annoyed customers to look for alternatives, cancel orders or start designing you out. It is also a gift to your competition of an opening into an established product sector. If so fraught with danger, should prices ever be increased, and under what circumstances?

The main reasons for increasing prices are: (i) foreign exchange considerations (i.e. appreciation of the $CDN vs. selling currency), (ii) the initial cost-of-goods sold (COGS) target was too low compared with today's reality, (iii) the business unit needs to make more profit (or less of a loss!), and (iv) you want to encourage customers to move away from an end-of-life (EOL) product to a newer version. No matter the reason, what is vitally important is how the decision is communicated to customers.

Some guidelines to consider are:

- Avoid changing prices on backlog orders (do it only for new orders)
- Give customers a reasonable notice period, and potentially allow them to stock up at the current price (conveniently, this can temporarily strengthen the order book)
- Support the sales team by ensuring that executives are available for calls or meetings if customers decide to escalate the decision
- Be prepared to negotiate with key customers if necessary – consider deferring price increases or keeping prices flat for strategic customers if the long term relationship is at risk
- Get your story straight, with solid facts, and ensure all customer-facing personnel from CEO on down deliver a consistent message
- Try to provide some sugar to coat the bitter pill: a new product announcement, improved customer support, enhanced co-op marketing funds, a revised volume-discount scale, a special promotional offer, extended payment terms, etc.

With the significant shift in the $US to $CDN exchange rate, plus spiraling energy and transportation costs, thinning profit margins for Canadian companies have made price increases relatively commonplace lately (your customers are probably doing it to their customers!). Just ensure that the long-term health of the business is considered fully before short-term price changes are implemented. If handled professionally, improved margins can be realized without damaging your customer base. Plan ahead and be willing to bend a little for the big customers. Like any delicate operation, price increases must be performed with a little finesse!

~ Joe Connelly ~

## *Implementing a CRM – A Corporate Right of Passage*

Most companies start off managing their customer interactions with Microsoft Outlook (or similar), spreadsheets and document templates. Over time, they realize that some form of Customer Relationship Management (CRM) software is needed. Here are some pointers to help you choose a CRM:

**Document Your Objectives**. To align the CRM with business goals, document the needs of Sales, Marketing, Customer Service, Finance and the executive team. The system must be aligned to workflow, easy to navigate and reports should be easy to create – or it won't be used.

**Develop A Requirements List.** You may not require a complex enterprise-level system. Some other things to consider before approaching vendors include:

- Hosted on-site vs. SaaS – Security, customization and integration with other tools are arguments for on-site hosting. SaaS offers scalable access and mobility with less reliance on the IT department.
- Porting of data – verify that help is available to transition your current data.
- Hierarchy and security needs – Multiple users addressing different regions/products may require data access to be segmented within the CRM.
- Integration with other IT tools – Ensure that the hooks are available to support different customer-facing departmental functions and to integrate with their current automation systems.

**Develop a Shortlist.** Besides the technical features and pricing of the product, what ongoing support is offered? Can they assist with integration? Will vendors be around in 5 years? Involve your IT department in the decision since you'll need them to support the implementation.

**Plan For Challenges.** Besides technical challenges, anticipate resistance from certain users. Some ways to increase the acceptance of the new CRM are:

- Schedule multiple training sessions and record them.
- Find a power user who can support other users.
- Publish a usage dashboard – nobody wants to be at the bottom of that list!
- Ensure executives lead by example by using the CRM themselves

The larger the organization and the more ingrained current workflows, the more effort is needed to implement a CRM. However, it is a corporate "right of passage" that can provide fresh insights into customers, more reliable forecasting and better conversion of opportunities into revenue.

~ Kurt Weber ~

## *Proposals – More Than a Necessary Evil!*

For most B2B companies, proposals are essential to the selling process and involve significant effort. The ability to generate winning proposals contributes to business growth. More proposals, with higher win rates mean more revenue, right? So it had better be a core competency of your business.

An effective proposal is more than just a price quotation. It is a custom sales brochure that creates a compelling vision of the customer's future should they choose your solution. It describes not only your value proposition but also the way you will deliver this value. They say you can't judge a book by its cover but customers will certainly judge you by the quality of your proposals! If the client hasn't worked with you before, they will use your proposal, and the interaction around it, as a proxy for what it will be like to work with you.

Keep in mind that your proposals and associated customer interactions are part of your "product"! This is especially true for professional services firms. So to win more business, don't just focus on the preparation OF the proposal; think about your preparations FOR the proposal.

An effective proposal process includes:

- Up front strategy sessions, based on customer interactions, that include making an explicit bid/no-bid decision
- Standard templates and "boilerplate" for consistent communication of value propositions (multiple versions based on the type of proposal) along with training on how to use them
- A clear, managed process for collecting inputs from different contributors within the organization
- A final review (a "ready to release" decision, just as you would for any product)
- Maintaining a repository of proposals as a source of valuable content, previous policy decisions and as a record of what was committed
- A win-loss review (including getting customer feedback on your proposal)

Not all opportunities are created equal so apply the right weight of process based on the importance of each proposal. But put genuine effort into all of them – if you don't really want to win it, you shouldn't bother bidding it.

Companies with better proposal processes win more business. They generate proposals that more accurately meet customer requirements. They also continuously improve their effectiveness based on their experience. Start implementing some of these steps with your next proposal. Before you know it, your proposals will become a competitive advantage, not just a necessary evil!

~ Doug Michaelides ~

## *Get With the (Strategic Accounts) Program*

Often when I coach a VP of Sales I get asked lots of questions about strategic accounts:

- What percentage of our overall business should come from strategic accounts?
- Should we choose a certain number for the whole company or some for each salesperson?
- Should we have strategic accounts for every product line?
- What criteria should we use to pick them?
- How often should we review and change our strategic accounts?
- Are all strategic accounts of equal importance?

The answers to these questions depend on the situation. But here are my guidelines for strategic accounts:

- Potential strategic accounts should be identified through a Marketing-generated segmentation analysis that isolates key players by market. This data should be filtered through your company's competitive strengths and weaknesses, then accounts picked with the best chance of long-term success
- Strategic accounts don't normally generate revenues immediately – typically it takes 6-18 months depending on your products or services and their sales cycle. So be patient
- Over time, expect 80% of your business to come from a select group of accounts – this helps stabilize your business in the long term. But if a single customer is contributing more than 25% of overall company revenues then you're in a risky situation
- Success at strategic accounts can reduce your overall cost of selling since it is often more efficient on a revenue/head basis
- Senior management should meet once per quarter to review strategic account plans, progress, roadblocks and funding. These meetings should help drive differentiation of overall service compared to non-strategic accounts
- The number of manageable strategic accounts is based on the resources available to properly service them. Picking lots of accounts and not treating them with "special service" defeats the purpose
- Avoid changing strategic accounts too often. I suggest an annual review with most staying on the list
- Since strategic accounts follow directly from a company's overall strategy, they must be linked closely with annual revenue targets and forecasted growth rates

To be effective with strategic accounts requires investment. You need a well thought-out and executed strategic account program to ensure they become a key factor in how large and how quickly your company grows. But it is worth it. Remember the old saying "To be a winner, play with the winners!"

~ Joe Connelly ~

## *Sales Efficiency On Steroids*

This is *not* another soapbox sermon about time management. There are literally thousands of books on that subject already. Those of us who have been in the business of selling for decades have already settled on our own "tried and true" methods of getting the job done. We have email. We have a mobile phone. But if we all have the same tools, what gives us that edge over our competitors?

To squeeze more efficiency out of your tools and processes, you have to put them "on steroids". It starts with spending a few minutes each day pinpointing when you are not producing but just doing busy work. Think about what you could do to improve your efficiency. Here are a few places to start:

- Is your Smartphone synchronized with your business email and contacts? You would be amazed at how many people answer "no" to this obvious question.
- Is your CRM software always open (on your desktop or Smartphone) showing you what is next on the to do list or are you shuffling through yellow sticky notes and loose papers looking for that scribbled phone number or name?
- Are there any customer business cards on your desk? Move the information into your contacts database and get the cards off your desk (and into the trash basket) so they will be with you all the time.
- When your desk phone rings, does it also ring your cell phone? This is pretty common technology now and allows you to remain available even when you are out of the office. (In fact, why do you still have a desk phone?)
- Are you making use of newer communications technologies like Skype, WebEx or GoToMeeting? Reducing travel means more time to book business. Odds are that your competitors are already using these tools to get a leg up on you.
- Can you tether your Smartphone to your laptop to give you Internet access anytime while you travel?
- How quickly can you locate items in your notebook? Are you organized by date or should you consider organizing by project or customer? There is lots of software (OneNote, EverNote, etc.) to help you do this.
- Is all of your collateral available and ready to send out (electronic and hardcopy) no matter where you are? Try storing it in the cloud on Dropbox.

The important point here is not the actual solutions (these will differ for each person), but rather to invest some time thinking of ways to better use your tools to step up your efficiency. This continuous improvement is what you need to stay a step ahead of your competitors.

~ Kurt Weber ~

## *Are Your Contacts "Orphans"?*

Have you heard of the term "orphan contact" as it relates to your personal contact database of names? It is not often used because people don't much like talking about it – especially people in Sales for some reason.

Basically an *orphan* is an entry in your contact database for which there is no "next action". Maybe one day in the future you might contact them. Or they might contact you for some reason. But who knows? Over time, you tend to forget all about these orphans so the chance of any future interaction (email, call, meeting, etc.) becomes very low. Their names just clutter up your database and obscure the important people in your life.

I know some people who like to boast about the number of contacts in their database as if this were some badge of honor. I'll ask them a few simple questions just to get them thinking:

- Why do you need so many names?
- How often do you actually contact these people?
- Do you have a system to regularly stay in touch with these people?
- Do you actively 'consult' your database when you need assistance in some matter?
- When did collecting business cards become such an important hobby for you? (ok, maybe that one is a little mean-spirited)

I try to prune my list of contacts at least once per year. I think of my contacts as a list of friends – I would rather have a smaller set of valuable friends that I can trust and rely upon, than a large number of acquaintances that I almost never speak to. Of course, I still have a pretty big list because, well, I'm a friendly guy.

Imagine for a minute that you've managed your contact database so that it doesn't have any orphans. Each name now has a next logical action (even if it is just 'call my brother in Scotland in 3 months'– which I need to do, by the way!). It's a much more focused approach and ensures more regular contact with the people you care about. The subtle implication is that you've now made a commitment to yourself to actively stay in touch with this list of people that will certainly enrich your personal and business life (especially if you are in Sales).

Plus, I think you'll find it's actually pretty cool to keep in contact with people you like!

~ Joe Connelly ~

## *Do You Follow Through on Your Swing?*

I am fortunate enough to live overlooking a golf course. One morning this summer I grabbed a coffee and watched from my deck as a number of players teed-off at the 5th hole. It was both entertaining and illuminating.

Some managed to hit good shots; some not so good. Some hit straight; some not so straight. After a while, I began to notice how few people actually followed through all the way on their swing. Everyone knows they should – it's one of the basics of golf – but not everyone did it. It is the difference between just playing and really being committed.

This got me thinking about taking actions and making commitments, and I wondered how well people follow through on all the "commitments" they make at work and in their personal lives. Sadly, particularly at work, many people don't do a very good job. Of course there are reasons for not meeting your commitments (yes, there are *always* good reasons!). In Sales, for instance, here are some of the many entries in the "Book of Excuses":

- It's no longer a priority
- I want to spend my time on more productive efforts
- I don't really think this action will be successful
- I just have too many things to do
- Damn, I forgot!
- I was never really totally bought-in to this action in the first place

There are many highly creative chapters in this book. Have a listen and see how many times in a day you hear someone (perhaps even yourself) quoting from it.

In Sales, as in life, you have to decide whether you're just playing or are really committed. Are you one of the few people known for following through, *every time*, on their commitments, or are you ready at a moment's notice with your own copy of the "Book of Excuses"? Maybe there's even an app for that on your iPhone . . .

~ Joe Connelly ~

## Doing Business in China? How's Your Guanxi?

The typical translation of the Chinese word Guanxi is "relationships", however it is more accurately described as relationships with mutual obligations, goodwill and personal affection. While Western business culture is often transaction-based, Chinese business culture tends to be relationship-based. To be rich in the West is to have lots of money. In China you are rich if you have a strong and healthy network of relationships.

As it has for centuries, even in today's globalized financial environment, very little happens in Chinese business without the effects of Guanxi. Of course Western business also relies on relationships and social standing, but it does not match the multi-layered Guanxi network in Chinese business. Any company seeking to be successful in China should have a conscious plan to secure its Guanxi.

In Western business culture once an agreement has been reached, or an order fulfilled, each party usually moves on to the next opportunity. The Guanxi perspective is to maintain the relationship long after the transaction is completed. More often than not the relationship will flourish even when there is little prospect of further revenues, sometimes progressing to a personal level.

Trading, operating or selling in China is challenging in many ways. Differences in time zones, language and business practices all must be managed. However it is having the right Guanxi that will ultimately determine success or failure. I have experienced Guanxi first hand on many occasions during my years in China. I see it in practice every day and have often benefitted from its power both professionally and personally.

There is no secret to good Guanxi. It is just about honesty, respect, doing what you say you will do and placing a high value on friendship and loyalty. Honest relationships are one of the age-old Confucian values. Chinese people would generally rather work with someone they know, or someone introduced by someone they know, than with a stranger, even if the stranger appears to have a more compelling proposition.

The more Chinese business contacts know about you, the more comfortable they feel and the more reciprocal Guanxi will take place. This is invaluable, but it must not be taken lightly. Once you start you need to continue to invest in the relationships even when there is nothing immediate to be gained. Good Guanxi takes time and has many levels; it cannot be bought, it cannot be rushed and it cannot be forced.

~ John Hartley ~

## *Sinking Exchange Rates – A Sales Nightmare!*

Canadian companies pay close attention to the ever-changing exchange rate to the US Dollar. Most companies selling products or services in the US (or worldwide) bill in $US and are subject to this constantly moving demon. I remember a time when my company increased revenues in $US by about 15% in a quarter, while the exchange rate decreased by about 16% (leaving us with lower $CDN sales than the previous quarter)! Until you have actually experienced the negative results of exchange rates it is hard to appreciate their full impact.

So, how can you minimize the potential negative impact of fluctuating exchange rates?

Start by getting alignment between the CEO, CFO and VP of Sales. This can be a complicated affair when setting the rate for the annual budget. Once agreed, it locks in the budget for the next 12 months and by default the $CDN sales targets.

Budgets are almost never revised to accommodate changing exchange rates. Sales organizations are usually challenged to "make up the difference" in revenues due to a negatively moving exchange rate. My advice (although it is tough medicine) is to hold your Sales organization accountable to deliver in the currency reported by the organization.

To mitigate the negative impact of exchange rate variation, companies can:

1.  Re-align expenses to be more $US weighted
2.  Place financial hedges (at a specific cost) to offset changing exchange rates
3.  Build exchange rate clauses into customer contracts
4.  Learn to accurately forecast geographic revenues over the longer term.

As a more extreme measure, a public corporation can be listed as a $US revenue company thus taking a large portion of the challenge away (this makes sense if most or all of the revenues are actually in $US). All of these approaches have varying degrees of success.

There is of course a potential silver lining. Exchange rates can move in the opposite direction too, yielding more $CDN revenues. This windfall should be considered "extra", with CEO and VP of Sales still driving for a higher "base number".

Oh the joys of the exchange rate rollercoaster!

~ Joe Connelly ~

TO HIS HORROR, GEORGE FINDS HIMSELF
TRAPPED IN AN ELEVATOR WITH A SALESMAN.

## *Do You Have A Killer Elevator Pitch?*

So, you've got 30 seconds to make an impression with a potential client, partner or investor: are you prepared? In my experience there are few people who have taken the time to develop the "killer" elevator pitch – the 30-second story of your company, product or service.

Consider how many times in your career you will have the opportunity to give your elevator pitch. It can happen at the most unexpected times, and is especially important when you first meet someone. I'll bet you will need to deliver that 30 second story THOUSANDS of times – so why not make it a real work of art that excites and motivates people?

An elevator pitch is a "short story" with a beginning, middle and an end. It should flow freely, and sound natural (not stilted) to the listener. It should be practiced until memorized and continually fine-tuned over time. Ideally it should be 'audited' by your friends, family or colleagues. It really is that important since you really do only have one chance to make a first impression.

Some questions to ask yourself about your pitch are:

- Is it free of technical jargon (normally a big challenge especially with technical people)?
- Do you include some reference to your target market (to help the listener frame the subject matter)?
- Does it convey possible benefits to the listener?
- Does it offer a few key "nuggets" of information that the listener is likely to remember (don't barrage the listener with too much information or you risk them 'switching off')?
- Does it include a call-to-action at the end (normally handled easily with an interesting ending question for the listener)?
- Would your mother understand it?
- Can you deliver your elevator pitch with passion? People will get excited if you are excited!

You are now armed with the basics of why an elevator pitch is essential and how to put one together. Try these simple 4 questions

1. Who you are.
2. What you do.
3. Why you're the best.
4. Your call to action.

Most importantly have some fun with it – you will use your elevator pitch a lot and the better you become at the delivery the more successful you will be – I promise!

~ Joe Connelly ~

# Are Business Referrals Worth the Hassle?

In the old days seeking new business was not done electronically, or even with direct marketing. It was done by "spreading the word". Professionals would get new business by obtaining referrals from past or current clients who were happy with their service or product. Nowadays with the onset of elaborate direct mail campaigns, automated CRM systems, a reliance on the web and social media, the art of "asking for a referral" seems to be on the decline. Here's why this is a mistake for anyone who is in Sales (and, by the way, when hunting for referrals EVERYONE in the company is in Sales):

1. Referral hunting is normally the cheapest way of finding new clients
2. People give up way too early in the process (it needs to be a process with multiple steps)
3. Some basic training is required (but not much!)
4. Everybody knows somebody who knows somebody who … (this is the whole idea behind LinkedIn)
5. Entire businesses can be sustained just through referral hunting

So what are the chances of getting a business referral the first time you ask someone? In my experience it is almost zero. People will commit to giving you a referral but most, for some reason, just don't seem to get around to it. So what's the next step? ASK AGAIN! The odds of success improve when you ask again a few days, or weeks, later (not dramatically but the chances are better). I actually use the 'Magic Rule of 3'. When you ask for a referral for the 3rd time, the chances of success go up significantly. By the 3rd "ask", people know you are serious and they are uncomfortably aware that they have made a commitment to you that they have not fulfilled. Be friendly and use humor in your requests, but be persistent.

They say that the typical Canadian knows more than 200 people. When you meet someone in a business environment, don't think of just that person but also of the other 200+ people they know that you probably don't. It pays to network and it really pays to ask for introductions or referrals consistently.

Of course it takes more than just asking. You need to earn the right to ask for referrals by building a reputation for delivering excellent value to your customers. But assuming you've built that reputation, how many referrals did you ask for in the last day, week, or month? Imagine if you were spreading the word about your business and asking for referrals EVERY DAY – yes, every single day. If you and your colleagues were to do this with EVERYONE you met, would your business have more high quality leads?

Try it – referrals are yours for the asking and it is most certainly worth the hassle!

~ Joe Connelly ~

## *Making the 80/20 Rule Work for Sales*

The 80/20 Rule states that 20% of your effort will yield 80% of your results. This shows that return on effort is disproportionate in nature. Successful sales people understand the impact of this rule when applied to their time and their business. Yet why do so many sales people not consider this rule on a daily basis? My guess is that there are a few reasons:

1. Most sales people genuinely want to help people. It is really hard for them to say "no" to a prospect even if the opportunity is small.
2. Salespeople are inclined to "go after everything" (i.e. don't leave a single order unturned)
3. You never know if a small order today will lead to a big customer with a big order some day.
4. Satisfied small customers with small orders might 'refer' you to other higher potential customers.
5. Your reputation could be impacted if you don't go after every order for every customer.
6. It feels like a gamble to go after just the bigger orders, so let's play it safe by going after everything.
7. It's too much work to go after the bigger, more demanding customers.

Sound familiar? Effort is not always just about the size of the customer or the order. It also includes commute time to a customer location, preparation time for one customer vs. another, an understanding of the account and its potential, etc. Some ways to make the 80/20 rule work in your favor are:

1. Make time management a critical skill that must be mastered.
2. Apply time (and thought) to where orders actually come from, their size and ability to be repeated.
3. Focus on the right opportunities so that time does not become the barrier to higher revenues as it is with handling lots of smaller customer orders.
4. Pick the customers that have potential both now and in the future.
5. Become skilled at identifying and going after the bigger orders (you decide where to play, so why not decide to play in the big leagues?).

Follow this advice and chances are high that your revenues will grow significantly (remember I am not suggesting to say "no" to all small customers, just choose them wisely and don't let them absorb all your time).

My personal experience of coaching senior sales executives is that time is a constant adversary that few master. Those who do will set themselves apart from crowd! Why not take 30 minutes at the start of each week to really think about how to apply brainpower rather than brawn to increase your revenues and success?

As someone once asked me "If you can spend a day to get a $10,000 order, or spend a day to get a $20,000 order, which day would you most like to replicate?"

~ Joe Connelly ~

# *Is Good Forecasting Actually Possible?*

*"Persons pretending to forecast the future shall be considered*
*disorderly"* – New York Crime Code

In today's changing markets, forecasting is becoming ever more important. "Time to expand", "steady as she goes", or "time to batten down the hatches", are just a few of the key decisions that are fed by the forecasting engine of a company.

Are you on the "forecasting is an art and not a science" side of the debate? I believe forecasting is a combination of reliable, process driven systems, tools to summarize the data, and most importantly, the proper interpretation of the data. This is a combination of art and science and relies on both the experience of the forecaster and the ability to see trends in numbers. Good forecasters will always listen very closely to their 'gut feel' as this often is a signal to dig deeper into certain aspects of the forecast.

It is also important to catch patterns in forecasting within a company. Examples are 'salespeople always forecast too high', 'big orders always come in later than we expect', and even 'we can never seem to forecast the last few weeks of the quarter'. All of these sound quite like systematic problems in the methodology and can normally be solved by a detailed review of the system, an understanding of the compensation model of the staff who are forecasting, management 'pressures' on the sales organization and a whole host of other more specific areas than can cause a 'consistent error' in forecasting accuracy.

Ever had to forecast in Canadian Dollars when customers buy in local currency (e.g. US Dollars)? I remember in the past having the challenge of trying to grow revenues faster than the negative changes in the exchange rate. With today's US/Canadian exchange rate hovering around parity it is wise to get the CEO, CFO and VP of Sales aligned as to forecasted exchange rates over time.

Of course forecasting will always have a degree of variability, so management needs to be clear on what level of accuracy is actually required by the company to run successfully. A closed-loop system should be put in place to measure and monitor performance, and corrective actions applied when accuracy falls outside a pre-determined range.

So, go on, set a forecast accuracy target and start measuring yourself against that accuracy – it could be quite illuminating!

~ Joe Connelly ~

# V.
# Innovation/Intellectual Property

## *Provisional Filings – A False Sense of Security?*

Your team has developed an innovative solution or significantly improved your product with a novel process. The approach has been tested and will be implemented in the next product release. Everyone agrees that the solution has never been used before and, as a significant differentiator, ought to be protected by a patent.

So you quickly document the solution and file a provisional application. This is cheap (~$500) and does not even require a lawyer! You breathe a sigh of relief. Your solution has been protected and you can forget about the patenting process for a year.

A year later, you ask you patent lawyer to draft a conventional application from the few pages you originally filed with the patent office. It turns out that 15 more pages must be added to properly describe the invention in order to write enabling claims! Worse still, you learn that only claims in which EACH element was FULLY disclosed by the provisional application will bear the date of the filing of the provisional application. The other claims requiring the additional disclosure will be dated with the filing of the conventional application. Sadly, you may have lost a year of protection by neglecting to disclose some minor details that, although not at the center of the invention, are necessary for it to be enabling!

If you really think your invention is worth patenting, I recommend that you do it right and dedicate resources up front to work with a lawyer to file a complete specification and claims. It is only through the process of writing the claims that you can ensure your description is complete. You may still want to file a provisional application initially (to allow for completion of testing), but at least you will know that you have secured the earliest filing date possible. Better safe than sorry!

~ Natalie Giroux ~

## *Married . . . With Intellectual Property*

So your company has cooked up a new product idea just ripe for the market. You've found the perfect partner to help execute the project. Everyone is pumped about the potential for success and eager to get the project off the ground.

Odds are that you were careful to sign NDAs with the various potential partners you evaluated including the one you selected so it should be safe to go ahead, right? But wait! Before you go any further, you need to establish who owns the intellectual property (including know-how, trade secrets and other non-patentable ideas). In fact, before meeting with any potential partners it would have been safer to define clearly what IP you are bringing into the project ("background IP" in legalese) to avoid any ambiguity. Your partner will also want to clearly identify what they are bringing into the project. Make sure you do this before you start talking about your big idea!

Once the background IP of each party is spelled out, you then need to agree on who owns the IP "jointly created" during the project. Even if you are paying for all the development you won't necessarily own the rights to the IP unless it is agreed upon upfront. You should also agree who will prosecute patentable inventions (filing, examination, maintenance and other fees), who will be allowed to license the patents when issued, who will get royalties, who will decide the inventorship, etc.

There's a lot to think about but take the time to document things before the project gets underway. Once the inevitable project speed bumps occur (delays, technical problems, cost overruns, personality conflicts and so on) the tensions in the partnership make IP discussions a lot more difficult. And as the prospects for financial success of the project become clearer, the stakes get higher. The last thing you want is to have your product launch stalled by expensive legal proceedings to sort out IP ownership!

You wouldn't get married without having an honest discussion about where you want to live, how many children you'd like and how the family finances will be handled – a joint venture project should be no different!

~ Natalie Giroux ~

## *The Joy of Cooking . . . Your IP Portfolio*

If you work for an innovation-based company, your company likely has a portfolio of one or more patent families consisting of applications filed in one or more countries. As the portfolio grows you must adopt the right approaches to "cook" it to perfection. Just as different cuts of meat are cooked differently to obtain the best flavor and tenderness, each application in your IP portfolio should be treated individually to achieve the company's overall IP objective.

One recipe is to "slow cook" an application… in this case you wait until near the 3-month deadline to answer an office action. You might even consider paying the late fees to further delay the expense of writing and filing the response. Be aware that this strategy will also delay the issuance of the patent, possibly by many years. This might makes sense if you have sibling applications (from the same family) being prosecuted on the fast track (see below) in another country like the US. The results of the US prosecution once completed, can be used to speed up the other applications in the family.

The other recipe is to "microwave" the application. In this case, you answer each office action as soon as it is received. In the US, if you respond to a final office action within 2 months, the examiner is also required to respond within 2 months, saving a considerable amount of time in the prosecution cycle! There are other programs available to speed up the examination process, such as the green program (which applies to inventions related to green energy and environmentally sensitive products) or the Patent Prosecution Highway (PPH).

Another very effective way to accelerate prosecution is to discuss an office action in person with the examiner. It is now possible for patent lawyers or patent agents to book face-to-face interviews with the patent examiner in Washington, to discuss his findings and explain differences between the application and the cited art. This process can significantly reduce the churn of office actions required to obtain a patent, shortening the prosecution time and lowering costs. Inventors may also be allowed, in some cases, to participate in the interview to provide their expert opinion on the differences between their invention and the cited art.

The "slow cooker" and the "microwave" approaches are at the extremes of the spectrum. Remember that each application should be treated individually to decide on the best prosecution strategy. For a larger portfolio, organize it like a recipe book – by dividing it into several categories and selecting the right strategy depending on the category. Happy cooking!

~ Natalie Giroux ~

## *Does Your Company's Hierarchy Stifle Innovative Thinking?*

*"The best way to have a good idea is to have a*
*lot of ideas."* – Dr. Linus Pauling

In most innovation-based companies, the CTO, architects or senior designers are relied upon for the key innovations driving the business. Because of their experience and positions, innovative thinking and problem-solving are expected from these employees.

Unfortunately younger, lower-ranked (but no less creative) employees, including the most recent hires, are often afraid to speak up about their own innovative ideas. To encourage more widespread innovation, these individuals must also see that their ideas are welcomed even if they are not immediately applicable or implementable.

One way to make the work environment more conducive to innovation from all employees is to hold regular brainstorming sessions. Open the floor to all staff for solutions to problems or ideas to improve existing products. It can be serious work, but have some fun with it!

Another good way to incite more employees to think outside the box is to award an "innovation prize" on a regular basis for the best new idea. The prize can be as simple as a plaque that moves around the office and can also be accompanied by a nominal gift (e.g. gift card). Again successful ideas need not imply something patentable, just some new thinking that advances your company in some way. Recognition by peers and management is an important motivator, particularly for new staff members trying to make a name for themselves.

To encourage the expression of innovative thinking, some companies have implemented anonymous internal invention disclosure processes for patentable subject matter. Employees can submit invention disclosures through an internal web site or through a colleague that is not involved in patent selection. Invention disclosures are periodically judged strictly on their value without consideration for the rank or position of the inventor. If the invention is deemed implementable or patentable, then anonymity is lifted so the employee can benefit from having originated the idea.

However you do it, imagine how successful your company could be if, rather than relying on tired solutions from the same old soldiers, every employee was encouraged, inspired and rewarded to think creatively to solve problems.

~ Natalie Giroux ~

## *Keeping Your Innovation-Based Company Innovative*

Your company was probably created and funded because there was an innovative technology or idea that led to the development of a unique product or service that satisfies your target market hopefully better than your competition.

Once its first product reaches the market, a company frequently enters a mode of feature enhancements, customer support and quality improvement. For small to medium size firms, these activities usually consume the attention of the entire R&D and product management team and that of the CTO. There is so much to do in order to meet customer expectations leaving little time to continue to innovate.

Beware! It was Andy Grove, the CEO of Intel who said, "Only the paranoid survive". You need a healthy dose of paranoia that your competitors will continue to innovate and find the next gem that will transform your market landscape, overcome your strengths and surpass you.

If time is a problem, holding monthly lunch and brainstorming sessions with your team is a great way to find new areas to innovate. Invite all levels of the company including new hires. They often have a different perspective on things, but may not feel comfortable speaking out just yet.

Remember, innovation is not necessarily something that requires a patent. It could be a more efficient way of testing, a cheaper way to design or a more efficient code implementation. It could even be a better way to serve your customers.

Boards of directors of innovation-based companies should set innovation targets on a quarterly basis, similar to revenue targets, which will positively influence the company to maintain a culture of innovation.

A true innovation-based company innovates continuously. It does not simply accept status quo or wait until a good idea presents itself.

~ Natalie Giroux ~

## Be In The Know Using Patent Databases

*He who knows when he can fight and when he cannot,*
*will be victorious* – Sun Tzu

Patent databases are excellent free sources of information on whether there are existing technologies related to your new product plans. As you initiate the design phase of a project, researching these databases can offer huge insight into existing technologies, who the major players are in a particular field and who owns a technology. There are some good reasons to systematically use patent databases as a technical resource:

- **Gain competitive intelligence** – Although the patents are published 18 months after their initial filing, the technologies and innovations that your competitors cover in patent submissions provide insights into their R&D direction and possible upcoming product releases. Maintaining a patent landscape on each of your key competitors and possible partners can provide intelligence on their plans.
- **Ensure freedom to operate** – Searching patent databases provides a good assessment of your freedom to operate by ensuring that existing patents or published applications do not already cover the key differentiators in your products. Some proof of freedom to operate is generally needed during due diligence performed by investors or acquirers. If there is any doubt over the ability to operate freely:
    - Change the design to get around the patent. This is much easier at the conception phase than when you are into high volume sales!
    - Purchase the patent to have exclusive rights
    - Negotiate a license or cross-license

- **Monitor the activity in your field** – By maintaining a patent landscape of your key technologies, you can identify new applications that could interfere with your own pending application and file oppositions or re-examination requests. This can prevent the granting of invalid patents that could later haunt you.
- **Find technologies and solutions** – patent database searches can reveal improved solutions for your technical problems and thus reduce development times. For example, there is a wealth of patented innovations created by universities available to license, often at low cost.
- **Assess patentability of your ideas** – often it is tempting to file for patent protection without properly determining whether there is any prior art. Would you not prefer to know the chances of obtaining a patent before committing to the cost of drafting and prosecuting the application?

It is true that the first search may be a daunting and time consuming task because of the amount of information that will be revealed. But by selecting the right filters, and carefully organizing and parsing the information, subsequent quarterly updates will become a simple task that will yield significant rewards in competitive intelligence and improvements to your products.

~ Natalie Giroux ~

125

## *To Know Or Not To Know?*

*If you know the enemy and know yourself you need not fear*
*the results of a hundred battles* – Sun Tzu

When you buy a property or a car, you usually invest the time and effort to verify the ownership prior to closing the transaction. However, some companies invest large sums of money to develop a new product without determining whether the underlying technology already exists and is owned by someone else.

There is a school of thought, based on old case law, that searching patent databases can lead to willful infringement liability. Therefore some companies avoid performing any research on these databases. However, recent case law (MIT vs. Seagate) requires that the accuser show definite proof that the defendant has willfully infringed their patent, not merely innuendo based on the active searching of patent databases.

Furthermore, the USA Patent Reform Act (2007), which is at its final approval stages in the Congress, will require that the accuser formally notify an infringer and give the company time to respond. Only if the infringer continues to practice the invention and is found to actually infringe the patent for which it was notified, can it be held liable for willful infringement.

There is a wealth of information in patent databases that can be used to understand new technologies and solutions, competitive positioning and industry trends. More importantly, searching patent databases can prevent incurring costly patent filing expenses, can significantly improve the chance of obtaining a valid issued patent and will reduce the cost of the examination process.

So, when it comes to your intellectual property, it is good to know!

~ Natalie Giroux ~

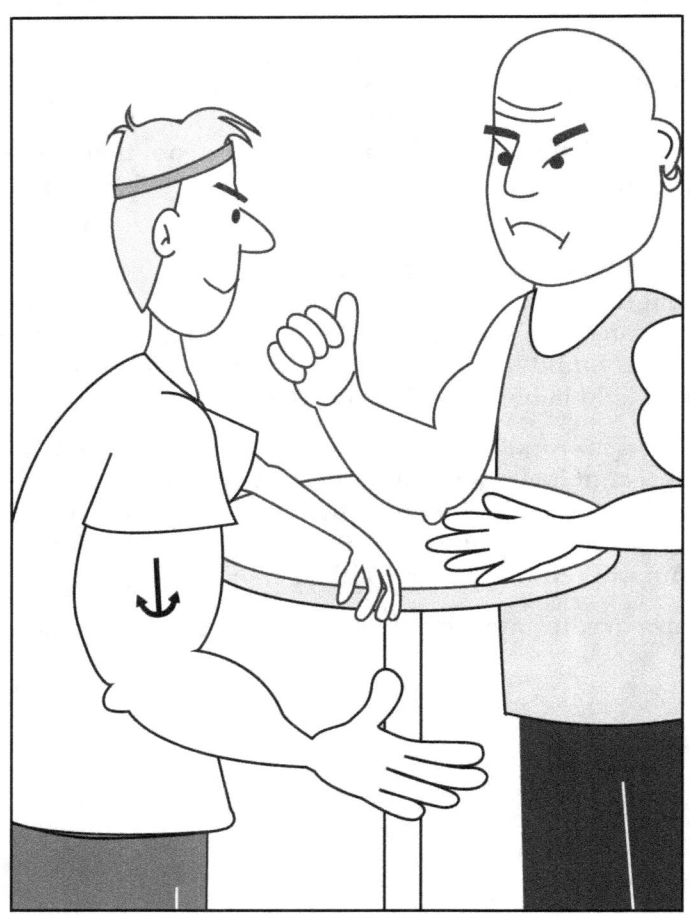

## *Does Size Really Matter?*

*What counts is not necessarily the size of the dog in the fight; it's
the size of the fight in the dog* – Dwight D. Eisenhower

There is a common perception that a bigger patent portfolio is better than a smaller one. In fact, this is often not the case.

Many licensing battles start by comparing the height of the pile of patents (Microsoft and Alcatel have more than 5,000 and 6,000 issued patents respectively!). For smaller companies, this game will never be won simply because of the cost of developing and maintaining a large patent portfolio. However, smaller companies can succeed in defending their rights using a single very strong patent even against large multinationals (e.g. i4i vs. Microsoft).

What is key in the development of a patent portfolio is to cover what you don't want your competition to do, and not necessarily to cover in detail how your product is implemented. In many cases using trade secrets is a much more efficient means to stand out from the competition. Regardless of the size of the portfolio, each patent needs to be written carefully and the claims have to be rock solid.

Inventors should be involved at all stages of prosecution to ensure that the required changes to the claims of the inventions do not detract from the initial intent. As the portfolio grows, it sometimes becomes difficult to maintain quality, so the company needs to rely on a good infrastructure to manage the process.

When it comes to patents, remember, what really matters is quality not quantity!

~ Natalie Giroux ~

## *Patent 2.0*

The recent phenomenon of social networking is now being used to improve patent validity.

An astounding number of issued patents that have gone through the scrutiny of examiners are found invalid by courts of law. It costs easily tens of thousands of dollars to obtain an issued patent, if one considers the cost for drafting, filing, maintenance and correspondence with the examiner. After spending this money, one would hope that the patent would actually be enforceable, but more often than not, a single piece of prior art unveiled to a judge can wipe out the entire investment.

To help with the process a new system is being implemented in the USA, referred to as peer-to-patent (see www.peertopatent.org). With this system, anyone can sign up to review applications voluntarily submitted by inventors, and contribute what they think is relevant prior art that should be considered during the examination.

This initiative, sponsored by the US Patent and Trademark office is in its third year and has proven its value by the growing number of reviewers and the amount of prior art uncovered. Large companies are using the system voluntarily to seek input on their applications. Other countries, like Australia, have now launched a similar program.

Here's a tip: even just signing up as a reviewer can bring insightful information about what is going on in your field!

~ Natalie Giroux ~

## Turning University Research Into Riches

How do we get more societal value from the billions of dollars spent every year in this country on university based R&D? While continuing to support academic freedom we must do a better job of achieving commercial benefits. Here are some things to consider.

### Timeframes

Most inventions take a surprisingly long time to get broadly deployed. Many of the core technologies in the iPhone were originally invented in the 1980s. The time from discovery to commercial success is frequently measured in decades. So, we shouldn't demand commercial output today from the dollars we've just invested but rather considering the funds we invested twenty-five or so years ago.

### People

One of the valuable outputs of university research activity is the highly qualified people. Many of these individuals find their way into industry. It isn't easy to measure the value that these people bring to our economy but this is certainly one of the key benefits we get from funding university research.

### Intellectual Property (IP)

One barrier to commercialization of research is the varied IP policies among universities. Most claim some right to all inventions made at the institution. Yet most Canadian university Industry Liaison Offices (ILOs) don't actually make any money. So why not allow the inventor to own the IP outright as a way to accelerate commercialization? This benefits Canada through the jobs and taxes generated. The university can also benefit from the bounty of these successful ventures. Think about how the University of Waterloo (one of the few Canadian universities to have adopted this approach to IP) benefits from RIM, Open Text, and DALSA.

### Cultures

To commercialize university research, we must bridge the worlds of academia and industry. Recently, one of Canada's leading research funders, NSERC, instituted a program that funds small industry-university collaboration projects. Programs like this reduce the cultural barriers to successful commercialization.

### Customers

Business people study the marketplace before launching a new product. Of course, at the earliest stages of university-based research, there is no market. But as we near commercialization, closer interaction with industry would help tremendously. So too would closer ties with business schools in the same universities.

We should be proud that Canada is among the world's leaders in per capita investments in scientific research. Without impinging on academic freedom or constraining discovery-based research, we can take actions to ensure the fruits of this investment have a bigger impact on our economy.

~ Jim Roche ~

133

## *Harvest The Full Potential of Your Intellectual Property*

Spring has come early this year to everybody's excitement. We are all eager to work on our gardens so we can enjoy their beauty during the summer. Whether you are creating a new landscaping project from scratch or upgrading an older backyard, you need a good plan. It is exactly the same thing with your company's intellectual property (IP) portfolio!

Even if you currently have no patents but have some unique technology, it is a good idea to map out your business direction and what your competition is doing so you can identify the key areas that require IP protection. Don't just think short term; also speculate on the different long-term directions your company could take and how these could influence your IP protection. This approach could save you a lot of money by avoiding unnecessary filings while ensuring that you protect yourself in key areas.

Mind mapping tools (such as the MindMap software from MindJet) are excellent ways to provide a visual representation of your IP landscape in collaboration with your technical team.

Remember, the most beautiful gardens don't necessarily have the most flowers. They are the ones that were planned carefully from the beginning, thinking about the long-term growth of each plant, their ideal location and how they interact with each other and the environment.

To harvest the full potential of your IP investment, you have to plan early and maintain the plan in synch with your business strategies and long-term objectives.

~ Natalie Giroux ~

## *Mining The Intellectual Property Buried in Your Company*

*Innovation is what distinguishes between a leader
and a follower* – Steve Jobs

Innovation is what differentiates your company from your competitors. But do you and your employee know how innovative your company truly is? Are you fostering an innovation-minded employee base? When was the last time an employee came forward with innovative solutions?

Innovation can be in products, features and services but also in creating a better way to build the product or deliver it. If your employees do not proactively come forward with their innovative solutions, it could be because they don't know how to recognize them as such. Worse still, perhaps they don't naturally look beyond existing approaches to make things better, simpler and more efficient.

"Invention mining" sessions are an excellent way to promote innovative thinking. You should perform quarterly invention mining sessions with different groups of employees; not only the designers, but also those testing, manufacturing and delivering the product. These brainstorming sessions are very useful to extract and document the innovation underlying your product offering.

Don't just look at what has been implemented or designed. Also consider other potential applications for a feature or how something could be done differently if an alternate underlying technology were available. Often, we think that innovation needs to be complicated. In fact the best ideas are generally the simplest! As long as it is novel and non-obvious to someone skilled in the art, it should be treated as an innovation.

As they identify innovation, employees will start to understand the value of innovating and will take pride in finding better solutions. If you reward them by celebrating innovation milestones (the allowance of a patent for example) you boost their morale and encourage further innovation. Not only will you be able to protect some of these innovations but you will also end up with better products or services!

Inventions should be carefully documented and a decision should be made as to the best way to protect them. Remember that trade secrets are a viable and cost-effective alternative to patents as long as they can be effectively protected, since reverse engineering is legal.

You should also maintain an innovation "landscape" which shows where your solution (product or service) is innovative and exactly what is protected. Keep these ideas well organized and documented; they are very valuable during due diligence.

By fostering an innovation-minded culture, you will quickly see the benefits in your product offerings and your success in the market. Imagine the wealth of innovation that could be driving your company to the next level of success!

~ Natalie Giroux ~

## *Do Your Employees Understand the Value of the Intellectual Property They Create and Handle Every Day?*

*Without knowledge action is useless and knowledge without action is futile* – Abu Bakr

If your company is based on an innovative product or service, you probably understand that Intellectual Property (IP) is one of your most valuable assets. Unfortunately, your employees, who are tasked to create and handle it on a daily basis, may not have sufficient knowledge to protect it effectively. Without proper training several mistakes can be made in the early days that can affect the value of your IP portfolio in the long term.

Your employees need to understand, from day one, that simple actions or lack thereof can have both short term and long-term implications. For example, something as simple as what they do or don't write down can become your best ally or your worst enemy in the future.

Regardless of the stage of your company, it is important to develop a comprehensive IP policy, customized to your specific business and to ensure ALL employees understand it.

The following list provides some important actions that should be part of an IP policy which will make a big difference in the future of a company's IP portfolio:

- Maintain effective security in the work premise and on computers
- Proper classification and handling of classified information
- Careful use of appropriate "log books" or "lab books"
- Proper marking of IP assets ®, ™ or "patent pending"
- Immediate documentation of ideas in Invention Disclosure Forms and regular mining sessions to extract innovation in new features
- Careful use of standardized features that can be patented (See *Lucent vs. Newbridge Networks.* District of Delaware. 1999)
- Careful use of freeware and shareware code

By explaining early on to your employees how to protect your IP and its impact on your company value, you will foster an IP-conscious culture and your company will be rewarded by strong IP that becomes a valuable asset to be monetized in the future.

~ Natalie Giroux ~

# VI.
# Start-Ups

## Turning Start-Up Dreams Into Reality

*Karim and Bill have been friends since high school. While Karim earned an athletic scholarship that morphed into an executive sales position, Bill parlayed his undergraduate software engineering degree into a Master's degree. Bill has just learned that his position, along with his R&D group, has been "offshored". Karim can't seem to break through into upper management. In his last review, his boss noted that his sales talent "should not be wasted in management". They've always wanted to start a business together, and feel the time is right.*

This dynamic duo has an intense journey ahead of them. There will be days of euphoria and of despair. During the ride, they must develop corporate and product strategies while staying focused on execution. No easy job!

**1. BANG! Revenue, profit**
As soon as the starting pistol fires, it's a mad dash to revenue and then profitability. Don't get sidetracked. Don't forget. Don't slow down. Don't sleep. Get to revenue. Get to profitability. Go!

**2. Differentiate or die**
Karim and Bill need to understand their competitors' offerings then figure out how to differentiate. A common mistake is to compete on the same basis as everyone else (e.g. "ours is the best"). If Karim and Bill were to do that, their profits would quickly erode, just before they got eaten alive.

**3. Learn to dance with the numbers**
Strategy is rooted in the financial statements of a company. Karim and Bill need to understand what are the key financial metrics upon which the success of the company depends. For example, if they plan a subscription service, they'll probably need to finance the first few months for each customer. One of their barriers to growth will be the availability of cash.

**4. Customers first, but...**
No matter how good the product idea, it needs to be tested first with real, paying customers. On the other hand, Bill and Karim have to listen judiciously. Just because someone at a big company suggests a particular feature doesn't mean it is a good one. See point 2.

**5. Attract strong advisors**
Neither Karim nor Bill has done this before. One way to make up for this is to build a strong advisory board with people who can help keep them on the best path. Mentorship is the lifeblood of entrepreneurship.

**6. Locate the exits before takeoff**
Bill and Karim should discuss what they want to do with the company over time. Take it public? Sell it? Grow it as a private company? If they have an exit in mind, they'll structure the company accordingly. If they don't know, then run the company as if they wanted to take it public. That keeps all options open.

~ Jim Roche ~

## *Start-Up Growing Pains*

Listening to the entrepreneur giving a presentation on his start-up business, I could sense his excitement and pride with their success. After all, it was an incredible idea and they had executed the start-up phase flawlessly. You could feel the audience getting caught up in his enthusiasm. But when it came to the question period, some of his answers got me thinking.

This company is so busy dealing with opportunities and issues that it's difficult for them to recognize the signs that they've entered a new stage of their business evolution – the growth phase. I've spoken with a number of successful start-ups and there are some common indicators that it's time to manage the business differently:

**You've grown your revenues and your organization but haven't quite hit the breakeven point.** Be careful – you can't make it up in volume if you're continuing to add costs along the way! Once you've hit the growth stage you need to be making money at a reasonable level of sales. That means getting economies of scale in R&D and production plus using more efficient means of generating new sales. Effective marketing can provide a constant flow of leads that ensures you are making the best use of your sales resources. Think about alternate channels to market as well. Can you sell on-line, for example?

**Your objectives, if you've had time to set them, are solely revenue based**. Of course you have to meet your revenue targets – that's like breathing. But also set strategic objectives that reflect your broader ambitions for market penetration, product expansion, cost structure and organizational growth. When you're clear on your strategic objectives, you've provided important guidance for planning across the company and have set the tone for your brand and marketing message.

**Sales are going well so there's no time to think about marketing plans.** Actually, now's exactly the time to build on your early sales success with a solid marketing plan that keeps the leads coming in and enables you to tackle new markets. Remember, 'failing to plan, is planning to fail' when it comes to growing your business.

**You've hired your first marketing person but it's not working out.** Did you hire a junior person to handle marketing communications tasks when you really needed a more experienced marketer to define and execute the strategy? Either way, the marketing plan will help you determine what type of skills to hire and when.

Recognize any of these situations? If so, it's time to start running your business with a little more structure to ease the transition into the growth phase. Rather than creating bureaucracy, some much-needed process will actually reduce the level of frustration your team faces as it struggles to cope with success. And if you do it gradually, it won't interfere with the vibe of entrepreneurship that you cherish.

With proper planning, attention to your cost structure and go-to-market effectiveness, your short-term start-up growing pains can result in some very impressive long-term gains!

~ Sandra Pacey ~

## Selling Out and Starting Up

We often hear about local high-tech companies being bought, usually by foreign companies. There are inevitably opinions describing this as a loss to the region and to Canada. But is this really the case? Cisco established itself in Ottawa with the purchase of Skystone. Alcatel-Lucent acquired Newbridge Networks. IBM broadened its footprint in Ottawa by acquiring Cognos. All of these organizations have flourished under the new parent. Other examples include the acquisition of Lumenera by Roper Industries and the purchase of Semiconductor Insights by United Business Media (UBM). Both have grown since being acquired.

In these cases, it could be argued that the acquired company benefited from the buy-out. Moreover, the acquisition created wealth for founders and investors, many of whom went on to start up or invest in other companies. So are acquisitions good or bad? That's like asking if mothers-in-law are good or bad: it depends!

Many acquisitions happen because the acquired company wasn't able to get traction in the market. In that case, the acquired company may have been bought for the technology rather than the business as a going concern. In this situation, the local region probably won't benefit that much. On the other hand, had the company not been acquired it likely would have failed anyway. So, better to be acquired.

Some acquisitions leave local management in place or allow members to take on bigger roles. Not everyone continues to reside in town, but those who do develop a better base of experience and a richer network of contacts to offer to their next employer. The local community certainly reaps the benefits.

While individual acquisitions aren't necessarily bad, we certainly will be in trouble if we don't foster the creation of new companies. A recent study by the Ewing Marion Kauffman Foundation showed that in the US between 1977 and 2005 the only net new jobs were created by start-ups. While big, high-growth companies like Google and Apple create jobs, other large companies like Ford and GM destroy them. On average, older companies destroy more jobs (e.g. through layoffs) than they create. Only start-ups create more jobs than they destroy.

This means that we shouldn't worry too much about acquisitions *as long as we have a healthy start-up environment*. It's the start-ups that drive job creation. Acquisitions help feed start-ups with talent and money.

The good news is that there are many exciting start-ups today in Ottawa. These are supported by SR&ED investment tax credits and other directed programs like IRAP. What we lack is availability of angel and venture capital. Last year, VCs invested about half as much per capita as compared to the United States. Without this capital to fuel growth, local start-ups are at a disadvantage compared to their international competitors.

If only we could sell more companies, generating better VC returns and providing more experience and wealth for the founders and other investors!

~ Jim Roche ~

# VII.
## Finance

## *Why IPO?*

Many entrepreneurs have the dream of taking their companies from a start-up to one that is very successful and growing significantly. Part of that dream typically involves the company becoming public with its shares traded on a recognized stock exchange. Why do entrepreneurs dream of taking their companies public?

The public markets allow companies to raise an important amount of capital that may not be available to small privately funded companies. We have seen and read stories over the years of companies struggling to raise capital in the private markets. Executives with good strategies for their companies have inadequate financial resources to execute their plans if existing and new shareholders are unwilling to provide additional funding. The public markets may eliminate part of this risk, thereby allowing the company to grow to the next level.

Many entrepreneurs take their companies public as a mechanism to enable their initial shareholders to achieve some liquidity on their investments. Most investors in start-up companies make their investments expecting that one day these companies will have their shares traded on the public markets, thereby allowing them to sell their shares and reap a return.

Another benefit to being a public company is the increased credibility gained in the eyes of customers, suppliers, partners, employees and the community. Public companies tend to have more visibility within business circles than private companies, as many people perceive being publicly traded is one of the criteria for being a successful company.

The compensation of employees through a stock option program is generally more effective in a public company than in a private company, as employees can assess the value of those options through the movements of the stock price. Over the last decade, many employees in private companies have questioned the value of stock option programs, particularly as companies have struggled to close their next round of financing. Public companies therefore may have a competitive advantage when recruiting new employees.

Public companies whose strategies include growing through mergers and acquisitions have a significant advantage in using their shares as a currency for transactions. Once a company has become a successful public entity, it can go back to the markets for additional funding through the issuance of new shares to allow even further expansion. Many factors will influence the company's ability to return to the markets for additional financing such as its success in delivering on its strategy and expectations, the receptivity of stock markets to financings in general and the appetite of investors for the shares of the company. With the challenging markets of the last couple of years, we have seen periods during which very few offerings were brought to market, as investors had little interest in increasing their exposure to the equity markets.

Good luck to all entrepreneurs with a dream!

~ Norm Paquette ~

QUARTERLY SEC FILINGS

## *Think Twice Before Going Public*

With entrepreneurs once again having dreams of taking their company public and adding more cash into the bank, they should consider carefully the challenges of being a public company.

Once public, the governance structure of the company will require significant change, particularly if it was previously operated by a founder with little outside influence. As a public company, the entrepreneur will be required to establish a board of directors that will include a number of independent board members. Following the establishment of the board, a number of board committees will need to be created including an audit committee and a corporate governance committee. The board and the various committees will typically meet on a quarterly basis to review the financial results and operations of the company.

The financial results for the company, which were private in the past, must now be presented to the world at large including employees, competitors and customers. Each may use this information in different and unexpected ways. Along with the financial results, details of compensation levels for the top executives will also be made public as part of the annual filings with the securities commissions. The CEO and CFO will be required to certify quarterly that the internal controls were efficient and effective during the reporting period.

The filings as a public company will place an added burden on the finance team with the requirement for additional information such as the management discussion and analysis (quarterly and annually), the management information circular (annually) and the annual information form (annually). Filings will also be required for any material change to the business such as a significant contract, mergers and acquisitions, or equity offerings.

Other factors to consider are:

- The increased insurance costs, particularly if you are listing on a US exchange
- The challenge of short-term decision-making that may influence the stock price one way as compared to a decision having long-term benefit of the company that could influence the stock price in an opposite way. For example, many public companies are influenced by quarter end boundaries regarding product pricing and discounts
- The management team, and in particular the CEO and CFO, will be working with a new group of shareholders and analysts who will require more attention and time than in the past.

Becoming a public company has many significant benefits but entrepreneurs need to temper their enthusiasm and carefully consider all aspects of the decision before taking this big step!

~ Norm Paquette ~

## *Let's Talk About the (Business) Climate*

The recent wonderful weather in Ottawa (20 degrees C in March!) got me thinking about the climate. If you're like me, your enjoyment of these warm, sunny early Spring days is tinged by concern over whether this is just good fortune or a result of climate change. The thought that what appears to be good news may really be bad news in disguise, casts a bit of a dark cloud over the glorious weather.

There's a parallel with business. Many companies are enjoying improved financial results lately. They'd like to think it is the reward for fiscal prudence, hard work and superior customer value. The question, however, is whether this improved performance is simply the result of an improving economy. Sure, we'll take the gains when they come; but isn't the real issue how you are doing relative to your competitors? Are you gaining market share? Do you earn superior product and operating margins?

Mixing my metaphors, they say, "a rising tide floats all boats". In the case of your business, make sure that rising performance levels aren't simply due to global economic warming. It is time to invest in gaining competitive advantage. After all, the objective isn't just to stay afloat; it is to win the regatta. Or, in the words of Warren Buffet, "You only find out who is swimming naked when the tide goes out".

~ Doug Michaelides ~

# VIII.
# Time Management

NED TRIES A NEW HABIT

## *Nurturing Positive Habits*

*"We are what we repeatedly do, excellence therefore is not*
*an act, but a habit"* - Aristotle

I recommend the book, The Habit Factor® by Martin Grunburn. It details the importance of positive habits in helping to achieve goals. These techniques are good not just for personal achievement or improving health, but can be applied to executives trying to excel in their roles and grow their business.

As an executive, you set high goals for yourself and your company. But too often what is lacking are the small steps or habits that set the directions required to achieve these goals. One example of such a "habit" is a weekly reporting mechanism specifically related to a goal. Proposing the mechanism is easy, but maintaining it and ensuring everyone keeps contributing to it is what requires adopting a habit.

Another example relates to motivating your team. Developing the habit of having an impromptu talk with a non-executive employee on a daily basis can make a huge difference in team spirit, how each employee feels empowered and their overall sense of being valued by the company.

With focus, a new habit usually becomes a reflex within a few weeks – something you don't even have to think about. These positive habits are a powerful means to diffuse negative habits. Getting rid of negative habits through willpower alone is very difficult, but if you adopt a positive habit, you have a better chance of eliminating the negative habit relatively painlessly.

There is a free application for the Habit Factor® for the iPhone/iPad that can help you develop positive habits and track them. Although at first it looks like just another "to-do" list, it can be used to consciously develop positive habits that will quickly become natural actions in your daily life. Worth a try!

~ Natalie Giroux ~

## *Managing Your Time*

All any of us have to offer are our talent and our time. Our productivity is heavily impacted by how well we use the finite amount of time at our disposal. When we get overloaded, our business results suffer and we put stress on our family life and health. What's the secret to effective time management? Planning and awareness.

**Planning**
Planning should be performed along three time horizons: long term (say an annual plan), mid-term (quarterly or monthly) and short term (weekly or daily). This may be as simple as writing brief lists and reviewing them regularly so you properly allocate your time towards achieving your goals.

A plan sets boundaries. It states what you are going to do and implies what you are NOT going to do. Your plan defends your objectives from the influence of outside factors, including the whims of your colleagues.

Think of business as a contest of wills. Successful people in business (and in life, I suppose) co-opt resources to support their own agenda. As a business manager and leader, you must ensure that you primarily drive your <u>own</u> agenda rather than becoming a slave to someone else's.

The success of the organization depends on the cumulative ability of all employees to execute their complementary agendas. The time management challenge arises when others are driving your agenda more than you are!

**Awareness**
An efficient time manager learns to operate on two levels. First, be good at the tasks you perform (you probably already are). Second, analyze your performance on the fly to remain in control of your agenda and your time. Here I'm referring to something along the lines of mindfulness and self-awareness.

With so many demands on your attention, it is easy to become an automaton, mindlessly reacting to incoming stimuli (responding to emails, fielding telephone calls, handling queries from your staff, jumping when your client or your boss says jump, etc.). Wake up! Your time is precious. At every moment, even in the middle of performing a task, ask yourself whether this is really the best use of your time. If not, take action to get back to doing the important stuff in your plan.

Time management "wakefulness" is the continuation of the planning process from the short term to the immediate. It is your final defence in sticking to your individual business agenda.

This isn't easy! While there are simple tools for regular planning, *awareness* is the mental discipline of having your head in two places at once (simultaneously on the task and above the task). People who are good at getting results and controlling their time, do this naturally.

Almost every manager I know is a student of time management techniques (though few of us are A-students!)

~ Doug Michaelides ~

## *Time for Spring Cleaning!*

The sun is definitely warming up! The birds are singing and the excitement of Spring is in the air. We've made it through another winter…

The change of season is a great opportunity to do a little house cleaning. Why not use the spare time created by a shorter than planned conference call or a cancelled lunch appointment to tidy up your desk and go through "the pile"? You know, that famous pile of papers that has stacked up for weeks or months (maybe even years) that you always intended to "deal with later".

Grab a cup of coffee, put on some energetic music and sort through it. Most of it will end up in the garbage, some of it will get filed, but maybe you'll stumble across that great idea you had scribbled on a napkin, or an errant expense check, or a magazine article you saved because it was relevant to an issue you've been trying to solve.

With the advances in electronics, our physical piles of paper may not be as big as they once were, but we still have to deal with "virtual piles" – stashes of old non-acted upon or non-sorted emails – which may also contain some hidden gems.

As you sort through your piles, you'll relive some of the recent history of your work life. This will help you review and reprioritize and may even stimulate you to look forward to new possibilities for your work and business. There's nothing like getting out of your daily rut, at least temporarily, to get you thinking….

So take this opportunity to go through all your physical and virtual piles and see how many great ideas never saw the light of day! Once the "pile" is gone and the dust is off your desk, you can take a deep breath and enjoy the light of the fine spring day too!

~ Natalie Giroux ~

## Garage Management

Why is it that my garage makes me tired? It's a nice garage, as far as those things go. It's big enough and bright too. But the floor needs sweeping, the walls need painting and the clutter needs organizing. The real problem though, is that I've been meaning to do these things since Bush was President. The first Bush.

My garage is an "incomplete". It sucks energy from me. Every time I roll my car into it, I think, "I should paint that wall," or, "I should tidy up that pile of junk over there." It's like the stack of unread books beside my bed. "I should read those books." Most of us have incompletes in our personal and business lives. Each one is like a little energy leech. Doesn't it feel good to tick something off a to-do list? It frees up energy. Conversely, having an incomplete drag along on the list traps energy.

If an incomplete sucks energy, what can we do about it? Use one of the four Ds: **Do** it, **Delegate** it, **Dump** it, or **Defer** it.

The best is to just dig in and get it done. The next best is to get someone else to do it. Third best is to just forget about it – dump the whole idea. Another alternative is to schedule it for later but then really do it then (or else it becomes another incomplete).

I decided to divide and conquer my garage. I swept it on Saturday. I've hired someone to paint it later this month. I decided that I'm okay with the clutter around the firewood. And next Saturday I'm going to clean up the clutter by the door.

Ah, that feels good. Now what to do about those books?

~ Jim Roche ~

# IX.
## Work/Life Balance

## *Feeling the Pressure?*

Every day we feel the pressure to give more to our work, often at the expense of our well being. This is compounded by the intrusive nature of email, tweets and the web that don't adhere to "8 to 5" work hours. We try to work harder to stay competitive but before long, fatigue sets in, affecting our work quality and reducing our energy levels. It is a downward spiral as we get worn out both physically and mentally.

I've been there. Fifteen years ago I worked all day then well into the night. I missed events at my kid's school. My weight ballooned by 35 lbs. and my cholesterol levels were rising. A late night visit to the emergency ward followed by surgery was my wake-up call. With the changes I was then forced to make, I was able to reverse the direction of my own downward spiral. Here are the lessons I learned:

- Make time to invest in your health. For me it was running and biking. You may find walking, swimming, hiking or, for my Canadian friends, perhaps dog sledding or hockey. Stick to it so it becomes a habit. The CDC, WHO and the AMA all recommend a <u>minimum</u> of 30 minutes (and up to 90 minutes) of exercise per day. Sounds exhausting but I guarantee you will actually <u>gain</u> energy over time. I found that after a while I required an hour less sleep every night – so my net time investment in getting healthy was zero!
- Have the courage to manage your work in-basket by saying 'no' when appropriate. If you are asked to take on more work, respond by asking what should be re-prioritized in order to rebalance your workload.
- Give it your all at the office but learn to shut the work drawer when you go home. Don't bring your work home mentally when you really should be focused on your family. A friend summed it up best, "Be there when you are there".
- Leverage technology to your advantage.  Avoid the rush-hour commute by working from home when you can. Ask your boss – the worst he could say is "no".
- Work more efficiently. Look for ways to get things done faster – like making a phone call instead of writing a long-winded email. And, really, do you need to attend <u>every</u> meeting you are invited to?

Take it from someone who knows, this advice is win/win for you and for your business. You will have more stamina and your mind will be sharp and clear. When the time comes to tackle a daunting project that demands extra effort, you'll be in a better position both mentally and physically to produce the kind of quality results you expect from yourself.

~ Kurt Weber ~

## *Profit From Your New Year's Resolution*

It's been almost 2 weeks since the start of the year. If you're like most people, you kicked-off the year by setting some goals or making some resolutions. I'll bet that at the top of many lists is a resolution related to fitness or health. It is a common New Year's goal, but also one that is often quickly abandoned, usually for lack of time.

The other day, I was struggling with a complex technical issue. I had turned the problem upside-down and inside-out but just couldn't seem to find a good solution. Before wasting any more time and getting frustrated, I parked the issue in the back of my mind, laced on my running shoes and went for a great run through the beautiful winter scenery.

Now and then I lightly brought the issue back to mind and as my run progressed I was gradually getting clarity on it. While my brain was filling with powerful endorphins, I was unconsciously solving the problem! By the time I arrived home, I had two novel ideas to tackle the problem. I realized that this happens to me a lot. Most of the time while exercising I solve problems and innovate without even noticing it!

We often try to solve business or technical challenges by staring intensely at a computer screen or holding endless meetings. Doing these things feels like we are "working on it". In fact, it might be more productive (and innovative) to bring the issue along with us while exercising to let the power of the endorphins help reveal a solution. As long as we have all the knowledge required, all that's needed is a different perspective that links up that knowledge in a creative way.

There is a wealth of research that shows how endorphins improve creativity and assist in making better decisions. The good news is that you can get a shot even without doing heavy exercise like running. Yoga, stair climbing or power walking can also do the trick!

It's not always practical to jump up and leave the office to go exercising every time you have a tough problem to solve. But when you're stumped, try to leave earlier than usual and give yourself a dose of athletics-induced endorphins. Or, try getting up earlier and exercising before a big day of meetings. It will help you stay focused and contribute to maximum performance.

So fuel up by exercising and you'll find innovative solutions that will help your business and improve your health at the same time! Sounds like the kind of great idea I have when I'm running…..

~ Natalie Giroux ~

## *Being Happy*

Anyone who reads The Economist, NewScientist or any other weekly magazine, is familiar with the holiday ritual of working through the pile of back issues that have sat unread over the past several months.

Perusing The Economist, an article caught my eye entitled "*The U-bend of Life – Why, beyond middle age, people get happier as they get older*". Apparently a variety of research indicates that we start out happy in our late teens, become progressively more unhappy into middle age, then get a lot happier again as we get old. The results, corrected for income, country and education reveal a basic human condition: people are least happy in their 40s and 50s. We reach a nadir at a global average of 46 years old. The good news is, after that, we have happier times to look forward to.

Coincidently, in the December 27th issue of NewScientist, I read about Ray Kurzweil, an IT guru, inventor and futurist. He boldly predicts that if we can just make it to the year 2045, we'll be able to live forever. He envisions enhancing our bodies through biotech and nanotech then ultimately transcending biology entirely by uploading the contents of our brain into a computer or new body. He's already started extending his biological life through a regimen of a low-carb, calorie-restricted diet, exercise, lots of sleep and the ingestion of various vitamins and pharmaceuticals. He claims that his test results show that he's only gone from age 40 to 42 over the last 20 years.

I can only assume that since Mr. Kurzweil is doing his best to extend the years during which most of us are at our least happy, he's hasn't read the article in The Economist. Or maybe he subscribes to Dogbert's philosophy (stated as he tries to cheer-up a disillusioned Dilbert), "Happiness comes from comparing yourself to a reference group that is relatively worse off".

Dogbert, misogynist that he is, then proceeds to inform Dilbert that he should be happy because he is a *successful* member of the reference group. And that's not nothing!

So what does this have to do with anything? If you're an HR manager, think about trying to maintain age diversity in your employee population, so you don't end up with a company filled with middle-aged sad sacks. And maybe help your employees with their New Year's resolutions to live a fitter lifestyle by offering healthy food in the cafeteria and snack machines, or by encouraging staff jogging groups and subsidizing health club memberships.

And for all you middle-agers out there, ground down by the weight of your responsibilities at work and driven nuts by your teenagers at home, push through! In a few years, the world will look like a better place. In the meantime, you can either restrict your diet to 1500 calories a day and exercise like mad, or simply remind yourself that there are lots of less fortunate folks out there that wish they had what you already enjoy.

~ Doug Michaelides ~

## *Make Your Bed!*

Recently I was having lunch with a friend.

Last time I saw him he was pretty much in despair over the loss of his job and the career that had for 20-odd years defined him. He had gained a lot of weight, he was unshaven, his hair was shaggy and he admitted that he'd been drinking too much.

This time, however, his hair was neatly trimmed and he'd dropped twenty pounds. He looked like a new man. Being male, I immediately assumed he'd found a new girlfriend but in fact he'd just decided to regain control of his life (actually, his current girlfriend had given him a gentle kick in the pants and told him to get moving on reinventing himself).

When I asked him about the secret to his transformation, he said, "I've stopped drinking and I've started to make my bed". I thought he was being allegorical about the bed but he was serious. "I know it's silly but if I have the discipline to make my bed every morning, no matter what happens during the day, I know I've started things off under control. And when it is time to sleep, instead of the tangled mess of sheets I woke up to, I see that nicely made bed and I'm reminded that I'm taking control of my life". It made sense in a funny sort of way.

I know a number of people, including myself, for whom cutting out alcohol was the first step towards reclaiming control in their life. I'm not talking about people with drinking problems, just people who had gradually started to drink more than they used to as their life became more stressful and unsettled (like Tony Blair). Resisting the crutch of alcohol is the first step towards a healthier lifestyle that includes eating better and exercising. It takes as much self-discipline to break that end-of-day cocktail (or three!) habit as it does forcing yourself to eat salad instead of steak or spend forty-five minutes on the treadmill in the morning. But in each case you get the self-fulfilling benefit of taking care of yourself as well as the confidence gained by being the master of at least some part of your world.

We all know that the debilitating stress in our lives comes from the things we can't control. This helplessness grinds us down and can cause us to succumb in other areas of our life. But that's no way to live! Once you've licked your wounds, and flirted with despair, you need to build things back up. Start with the things you <u>can</u> control; your immediate surroundings, your behavior, your health and your relationships. Every step you take restores your confidence and prepares you for the next bit of progress.

As my friend said with his old ironic smile, "Now that I make the bed so nicely every morning, I'm inspired to start washing the sheets more often too!"

~ Doug Michaelides ~

www.ingramcontent.com/pod-product-compliance
Lightning Source LLC
Chambersburg PA
CBHW081447170526
45166CB00008B/2342